WOOD, WATER, AIR AND FIRE

The Anthology of Mendocino Women Poets

◆

WOOD, WATER, AIR AND FIRE

The Anthology of Mendocino Women Poets

◆

EDITED BY

Sharon Doubiago
Devreaux Baker
Susan Maeder

POT SHARD PRESS
COMPTCHE, CALIFORNIA

First printing November 1998
Copyright ©1999 Pot Shard Press
Manufactured in the United States of America

Quote on page 19 reprinted by permission of New Directions Publishing Corp. Denise Levertov: "Some Affinities of Content," *New and Selected Essays*, page 5. Copyright ©1992 by Denise Levertov.
Since this page cannot legibly accommodate all copyright notices, the permissions begin on page 321, and constitute an extension of the copyright page.

Design and composition: Elizabeth Petersen
Cover art: "View of MacKerricher." Dry pastel by Tamra Whitney.
Map art: Elizabeth Petersen

Publisher's Cataloging-in-Publication
(Provided by Quality Books, Inc.)

Wood, water, air and fire : the anthology of Mendocino women
     poets / edited by Sharon Doubiago, Devreaux Baker, and
     Susan Maeder.
         p. cm.
         Includes index.
         ISBN: 0-9656052-3-X

         1. American poetry—California—Mendocino. 2. American
poetry—20th century. 3. American poetry—Women authors.
I. Doubiago, Sharon. II. Baker, Devreaux. III. Maeder, Susan.

PS589.W38 1999   811'.540809287'0979415
                                QBI98-922

ACKNOWLEDGMENTS

Wood, Water, Air and Fire was the brainchild of my co-publisher and friend, Johanna M. Bedford. Her helpful eyes and hands have guided the publishing process from start to finish. Without the discretion of editors Susan Maeder, Devreaux Baker and Sharon Doubiago, this book would not have the shape Johanna Bedford envisioned.

The women poets of Mendocino responded generously to Pot Shard Press' call for their work. Our commitment to publish new poets and bring better-known poets to a wider audience has been rewarded by quality, diversity and depth.

Liz Petersen continues to bless Pot Shard with her expertise in all aspects of design. Donna Bettencourt and Mary Bradish O'Connor's proofreading and editorial skills rendered the book more readable. Tracy Porterfield's clerical support delivered the manuscript on time after Chuck Wilcher's computer wizardry rescued us repeatedly from ignorance.

Two important women in my life—my mother, Mary Gary Harrison, and my partner, Jane Austin Harris (who came up with the title of this book)—have given me the strength, support and courage to undertake this project.

I thank each named and anonymous angel who helped get *Wood, Water, Air and Fire* off the ground.

—*M.L. Harrison Mackie, Publisher*
Comptche, California
October 1998

CONTENTS

Julia Butterfly Hill

Susan Maeder

Kay Lieberknecht

Cynthia Frank

Sarah Flowers

Maluma Crone

Liz Haapanen

ruth weiss

Jenny Gealey

Mendocino is isolated by the Pacific Ocean and by miles of winding roads running through inland valleys or along the coast. It is three hours north of San Francisco, four hours west of Sacramento and six hours south of the Oregon border.

The beauty of its mix of land and sea is the setting for environmental activism in the face of historical logging and fishing operations. Tradesmen, hippies, artists and retirees coexist in small towns scattered throughout the area.

INTRODUCTION

All my life I've wanted to just speak truth, without posture, artifice. I've wanted out of hate, prejudice, mime; out of cliché, out of lies, out of program, party line, out of the bounds of this nation, the traps of societies. For years, I couldn't complete a single poem. And then, most surprisingly, Mendocino connected me to true story. There I found the story lines. Simultaneously, I found some sort of faith in common language, faith to attempt the untold and forbidden. In some overall way, *Wood, Water, Air and Fire* evolves, I think, from similar longing: to know, then speak, truth.

What the poet Denise Levertov learned is startlingly true of this collection. Northwest poetry—Mendocino being its southern border—is characterized by "a deep spiritual longing . . . (that) gives rise to a more conscious attentiveness to the non-human and to a more or less conscious desire to immerse the self in the larger whole—that element I have called the spiritual quest."

These poems are testimonies of entering the lives of others, other worlds and of being entered. Flesh turns into soil, shells, trees, rivers and ocean. Everything is breathing, has soul, is conscious and is story. Everything that has ever happened is still happening and being made visual in the branching, leafing and budding, speaking in the many sounds of water.

Criteria for inclusion in this book was defined by geography, history and quality. Pot Shard Press called for voices of all ages, wanting to publish a book that would represent women poets of the coastal area, their rich and diverse artistic talent and history. The sixty-three poets here range from "five days short of fifteen" to eighty-eight.

Mendocino was my last permanent address. I left when my heart was broken but I always go back, I always will, to sleep on the streets there, on the beaches and in the woods and be renewed in poetry.

—*Sharon Doubiago*
Laramie, Bandon, Ashland
June 1998

NOTE: An asterisk (*) at the bottom of a page indicates the continuation of a stanza on the following page.

Mary Norbert Körte

DO NOT TOUCH THE RAIN STICK

the year of great hippie migrations she wintered
in the woods & ever since   one by one years
merging into Douglas fir Pacific yew great Red-
wood Cathedrals as they say growing into one
another fed by blood of shadow mammals ridges rocks
down to bedrock wearing the river's roar   silent
mushroom mud   madness hiding inside scorpion's tail

she was secretly pleased   water ran so high
    it made her gasp & wow
pleased to walk into closed arms of trees
pleased to watch slow gathering of roots
pleased to think she might understand
speech of rain never-ending suss inside her soul

till she became angry at this thunder thrown
pushed against a smothering sky she cried
out for light lapping at the edges of her dark
hollow breath beating against moss
carried hard by transient stars

& moon laughed   told her she was a fool
for bringing home the rain stick even though
    she was gringa & it was tourista mercada
she should have known when it fell on her head

it would wake the rain inside it was time
to slide her down down that verdant winter
darkness down into rapturous debris

all those hillsides 25 years of hillsides
sliding out in a plume great plume

all the way all the way out to sea

Spring Equinox 1998

WOODEN WOMAN WITH HAIR

changes into a bird the way
she moves in and out of the eye

the way of wood ghosts
little people   the Daphne

this woman with wooden hair
she has lived here a long long

time blooming inside the eyes
of night creatures who see

she is a little goddess sitting
just inside the door over

there beside the mirror
the one who casts light

from the pure heart
to the river to the great trees

Fall Equinox 1992

EPISODE IN WHICH SHE EXPLAINS WHY SHE LIKES ART THAT MOVES

there a raven facing north—
west in the painting after
4 yrs appears this misted
in summer heat morning far
away far away from the raven
                on the wall

since she cut a hole in the woods
in good Anglo settler tradition
since she opened a meadow
songbirds have moved in
                no longer

✻

ravens dominate the trees they
have gone off the birds
who learned to stay high in the
Douglas fir that aren't there any more
robins & flickers of her prewar Berkeley
childhood have moved in singing
along with her 4 greedy cats

now birds want black cap
raspberries they pass up roses
for the geraniums and she
never knows when the next cat
will turn up the next canyon wren

she installs deer-proof butterfly bush
she listens to her friends when they tell her
beware exotics in the redwood forest
but the cats will die off as cats will
and she gives away Black oak inland
she ignores Scotch broom at her peril

where the raven flies in to the painting
this day sure & clear as the raven on the wall
they are both looking the same
                west north west
she keeps trying to figure out
what is the day's news

Midsummer 1996

LINES IN THE DARK

the neighbor children believe her
house is made of gingerbread

she wonders about this when
the neighbor & the neighbor's
children come to visit
she heats her house with the
*

wood cookstove oven all winter
long into freezing river falling
trees broken with frozen snow

she has been asked interrogated
the Hound of Heaven Truth
Are you   (well) are you
this we have dreamed this we have
feared are you this we have known
since the first life last life journey
down birth canal into the next life
as into vows as in virgins
embarrassed by summer's veiled world
gauzy stepping in tomorrow's dance

but winter stars crowd in on
her & her silence
like gawkers at an accident
they lead the neighbor children
to believe her house is made of
gingerbread they point to the ghost
in the trees & children climb
over her like a plague of elves
they come holding on to adult men
who then stand in her front yard
telling her what's wrong with the place
& drinking her coffee & drinking her
wine & drinking her dry of love
they never   never never see that
her house is made of gingerbread
& has been so for a thousand years

Midwinter 1992

Karin Faulkner

TREE BONES

There's a structure
    You can see it—map it out
graph it like statistics
    in black and white
        horizontal and vertical lines
    or draw it with branches
to make it look like
    a family tree.
        Pairs of people
           who came together
               and reproduced or didn't
           stayed together or didn't
        lived a long or short time
        and died.
        You can see branches of the family
      Grandparents aunts uncles
with all the cousins spread out
like finger bones from the palm.
        You may find the occasional liaison
         a genetic contribution
           irregular in the diagram
              one who came   caused a birth
             failed to marry
           but left
               a descending line
                 on the chart.
                   A child.

There's a structure
        that twists around itself
           like a spine doing yoga
             a helix serpentine
                 deoxyribonucleic acid
          ribbon of paired chromosomes
             river of heredity.
          *

You have a mother
You have a father
                inside you.
Looking through the window
of a microscope
                you'll see their structure
                the snaky curvy way
                                they built you—DNA.

Maybe it curves the way
the bodies moved up against
each other trying to feel
something through the skin
and deeper.

Maybe it curves
the way music does
singing the song
of the family tree.

STUTTER

The clock is stuck in the boy's throat again. The girl is frozen. The mother has started to grow huge with fear. The father smiles, thin-lipped because he doesn't know what else to do.

The clock got stuck when the word got stuck. The girl froze when the word got stuck. The mother grew huge when the word got stuck and the father smiled because he wanted it all to be normal and he didn't know what to do.

The word got stuck in the boy's throat. The girl is frozen with a serving bowl of mashed potatoes in her hand. The mother is growing huge with her knife in a piece of meat. The father smiles into the middle distance.

The boy begins again. The steam rises from the mashed potatoes into the light hanging above the table. The knife blade moves across the meat fibers, severing them. In the middle distance the father smiles at a memory.

The boy tries again. He knows the word he wants to say. The girl knows the word he wants to say. The mother knows the word he wants to say. The father knows the word and wishes the boy could say it so everyone could come back.

The boy tries again. The girl's hand cannot hold up the heavy bowl much longer. The mother's knife has reached the plate. The father is playing touch football with his brothers when he was the same age as his son.

The boy tries again. The girl wishes she could leave her body like the steam leaving the potatoes. The mother wants to take her knife and cut the tension wrapped around her neck like a snake. The father has caught the ball and is running.

The boy tries the word again. The girl moves her other hand and uses both hands now to hold up the bowl she is trying to pass to her father. The mother's hand is in the air holding the knife. The father is running faster than his brothers.

The boy tries the word again. The girl imagines she is offering a baby in a bowl to her father. The mother imagines she can cut the word free from her son's throat. The father imagines he threw the ball into the sky and watched it disappear forever.

The boy tries the word again. The girl mixes these thoughts with the steam, "If there were a God he would free me, but there is not." The mother recalls the doctor drunk the night her son was born. Her mouth suddenly tastes like metal. The father notices a perfectly cloudless sky and smiles.

The boy tries again. The girl wants to scream and break the bowl. The mother wants to kill the doctor with a steak knife. The father wants his brothers to catch him.

The boy tries again. "Re," he says. "Re," is all he can say. "Re," again. Sister, mother, father all look at his mouth by only moving their eyes. Forever. This lasts forever.

Remember. The word is Remember.

ON CUTTING THE FRUIT

What has brought us here
nearly a decade from our first decisive act
to this point in the kitchen:
She stands, or I stand depending on point of view,
before the kitchen window
knife in hand,
one perfect pear on the cutting board
and finds herself unable to eat
a bite or all of it
without offering half of it
to you?

There was no kitchen in Eden.
Someone may have watched her though
if not through a window,
then between the leaves in that garden,
as she stood naked
and full of her own individual hunger,
one perfect apple in hand
and looked around her for Adam.

LANDSLIDE

"Part of the trouble is that I've never properly understood that some disasters simply accumulate, they don't all land like a child out of an apple tree."~ Janet Burroway

How many slightly closed doors
brought us here, my love?
How many half-conversations?
How many innuendoes and resentments
congealed cold on their serving platter?

How many swallowed intentions,
unnoticed generosities?
How large a population
of partly revealed selves?

It was a long, slow cadence—
part dirge, part sun-lit sonata.
A melody so subtle it got lost in the kitchen
or shut in the garage
or left to mold in the bottom of the fridge.

It was an accumulation of omissions,
of unspoken promises unkept,
of incomplete revisions—
and not the surprising disaster
of infidelity, brand new love
or announcement of the urge
to go abroad alone.

Not an avalanche caused by all the anger
exploding spontaneously at critical mass.
No, just accumulation. Like all the water
now held in these hills
which begin their slow slide
to the bottom, pulling rock, tree
even house down with it
as it closes the road.

I never properly understood
that tolerance for pain
tolerance for hunger
welcomes these accumulations,
like grease attracts dust,
like the first dirty dish in the sink
invites all the others.
I never understood that a hopeful stance
is the perfect posture
for holding up the weight of the world

The sudden calamity announcing,
"The end of all this!"
was what seemed written in this,
as in every Hollywood movie.
A break, clear as lightning
in the continuum of our intimate darkness
Not this slow silent landslide
that seems to want to take us, my dearest,
all the way down.

DÉJÀ VU

We have all been here before.
It's not a radical new idea.
Who am I this time?

Or are we living several lives at once
full of déjà vu breakthroughs?
We have all been here before.

If the soul lives on
recycling through many lives, many bodies,
who am I this time?

I've got bits of my history with me.
Old loves and deaths in my pockets.
We have all been here before.

We meet each other again facing
the other way on an old path. Do you know me?
Who am I this time?

So time is like a screen door, a two-way mirror,
a three ring circus—past, present and future.
In one ring someone tries to tame lions.
In another a pretty girl stands on a running horse.
The third is full of clowns
with big feet and little cars.
Who am I this time?

I'm on this tightrope strung high over all three.
Worried about balance.
Past, present and future. With no safety net.
Look up. I'm waving. Don't you recognize me?
We have all been here before.

Zida Borcich

INDEPENDENT TRIALS

Give me the name of that law again, Moe,
I'm so bad with names these days.
The Law of Undiminished Chance, was it?
Oh, they swear by it here, wear it on their eyes.
Was it the Law of Interminable Deception?
The one that applies to slot machines
Where the old ladies sit holding up their cigarettes
Like movie stars they used to watch, and push and push
And feed the coins, mouths set, into the little flat hole.
After a while their mouths resemble the slot so much,
And their yellow, rumpled skins, their printed blouses
With dissatisfied flowers, practically yell how much
They want to escape but don't have the will to make the move.
Wasn't it called the Law, the Law of Something?
I know you remember. Law professors always have
The names of Laws on the tips of their tongues
And call them out like memories, jogged by the looks
On the desperate faces who've been here awhile,
Or the newly arrived hopeful faces,
Or the beaten down cab driver faces
Who used to be show girls till they got too old
To look the way they should, and keep a lot of stories
Packed tight in the lines on their cheeks.

That blonde's about my age, combing her hair in the mirror
And having her martini for brunch. I'll see her again at 21
Ineffectually flirting with Frank and giving her money up.
By three, a homely guy will beg her to go upstairs
And they will practice the Law of Numbed Debate.
Takes their chances and pays their price
For the privilege of extracting a little of that Wayne Newton fun
Outta this Wayne Newton kinda town.

The Law of Desperate Wagers, Dissipated Wages?
I can't think. I can't think in here
*

With that plunking of quarters hitting aluminum bins.
It's a din—a *din of inequity*, I say!
And what is that bad arcade music tootling again?
Too bad the artists who design computer music have no talent.
They are ruled by a Law called Artistic Blanching.

That man over at the poker tables just put his stomach
On the chair next to him and had the dealer
Pass it a hand and it won, and the other players
Grumbled that it wasn't fair to lose to a body part.
But hey, that's Vegas, right?

Brides, immense and expectant, rolling of gait,
& starry of eye,
Surrounded by their families, the hapless grooms,
Hold up their long white veils, hold up their trains,
On their way to the Chapel of Anything Goes—
Through the casino and to your right!
The invitations read, "You are joyfully invited
To share our joy at the joyful marriage
Of our daughter
Joyce
At Circus Circus."

I can hardly breathe in this place!
I can't see with all this smoke. It's too glittery here
And I can't distinguish between revulsion and frogulsium.
That Law must be at work. And there's too many people!
If I could just go outside I'd remember the name.
But I have this feeling right now, this big feeling . . .
If I go, I might miss the big one, but there's . . .

Something . . . something about the Law, the Law that says
That after two hours or six hours of feeding nickel slots,
Quarter slots, dollar slots, cherrybarbarseven slots,
There is exactly the same chance of hitting
As in the first minute.

So you can move, Mom. Don't even tell the lady
To hold it for lunch. It's not due to hit, see,
Just because you've been sitting there since yesterday.
But what a shame.
That's some law you got here.

PUNDIT'S

If that RV hadn't run into my door
I never would have found
Pundit's Body Shop & Free Verse
Alongside the Spare Time Vacant Lot on the highway where
Fatboys played languid games of baseball,
Spitting and scratching their butts all day
Just like the ones on teevee do.

They came over to Pundit's to lean above the squirting arch,
Gulping as it gushed from the warm hose,
And to piss behind his shed. Adjusting their balls,
They stood awhile watching and listening
Before they went back to the field.
Gape mouthed they listened to him,
Tried to suck up his wisdom
In the hot greasy Bond-o white-lit afternoons.

Pundit? You Pundit?
"Is the Pope Polish? Huck."
He laughed, raising up his shoulders w/each huck.
His hairy belly poked out under the
Filthy white tee shirt and when he turned
You could see the crack of his ass
Above the shapeless, crotch-lagging jeans.
The buttocks looked like loaves of bread.
A can of beer was not far off
And he smelled like sheep dip.

"No BATTA. No BATTA."
Piping fatboy voices came over the weeds as slow
As the speed of sound in a hot summer—
Way slower than the winter speed and farther off, too.
"Yep. Looks like a squeeze box, got squoze.
A accordion sidecurtain. Take a week ta fix."

His teeth looked like a bowling spare.
His eyebrows seemed to sprout like carrot tops
In odd directions, rank and greasy.

Harmlessness was like a bumper strip
On his round cheeks and stubble—his slogan, like
Baby on Board   Ex-wife in Trunk   My
Other Car Is Up My Nose.
An unconscious and deep-running kindness
Drew to him the lame, weak, unpopular and misfit.
So he kept a pot of coffee boiling endless on the burner
By his desk and served it to all the bums who came there.
His tortured fingers tipped the pot with awkward
Friendliness as he listened to their lies,
Pouring the burnt stuff into overused styrofoam cups.
And wasted time was part of the deal, too,
As he had to turn off the sander sometimes
So he could hear them all.
He had to quit thumping the metal to hear them.
He had to come out of a tight spot to look
Deep at their faces and listen.
His wisdom was a listening that had no judgment to it.
His was Pundit's Body Shop & Free Verse
And there was no sophistication in it, no psychology exactly,
There was no conflict. There was no sneer there.
There was no mall, no music video, no attitude.
There was no one measuring or keeping score—
Only the ease of listening without advice to give.
Pundit's
Met their needs without a ploy or motive
In the particular stink and temperature
Of a place like that.

ODE TO A PRINTING PRESS

O Press!
O Heidelberg that swings
While at the same time
Squats, solid & black
& shining.
Your windmill arms
Flash and flick, crack
*

& whip around a breeze.
Your flywheel sings
A bass beat.
(That little tear in the belt clicks,
Repeats, clicks, repeats.)
Your gears chunk.
Pneumatic song you sing,
The whirling mesh of
Bearings
The suck, the swoosh,
Wheezy exhale of air blast,
The Pump, the low tones,
The hush between.
The thump of paper to type,
The hiss of ink between
Form rollers & drum,
The fountain a metronome,
Feeding color to the page.
Crisp rap of paper
Flipping round,
Delivered
Picked up
Delivered
Picked up
Delivered
Light, clipped, rotating,
Giving voice
To someone's dream.
Words, meaning, definition
(Distinguishment   Style   Typographic)
Keep those cards and letters
Coming.
Windmill
Windmill
Heidelberg
Windmill
Windmill
Press Press Press
Rhythm & Blues
Rhythm & Reds
*

Rhythm & Blacks
Meaning in the sheet
Meaning in the printer
(Platen Tympan Forme Bed)
Squatty black elegance:
A German machine:
No screws,
Tapered pins
And harmony of use.
"Work taken to extremes
Describes love."

DARK PLACES WE HAVE NOT FAR FROM HERE

I am on a bus on 54th Street.
New York City looks a little lost &
Down-at-the-heels on this end of town.
I turn my head and watch a little crab-like man
Scuttle up the stairs of a red place.
The sign says, "Stark Naked Girls."
I think about what he will do up there,
Think about poor old Peewee Herman,
The human condition that wants something
So bad that a whole place, an entire city
Has a feeling of being hungry.
They want something so bad
But they don't know what it is.
(Do I have it? My life works, right?)
I get down off the bus. I have to walk.
There is grime on the street
I know will not come off,
And it adds to the atmosphere of wantingness—
Things blowing down the street, the sound of trucks.
There is the clump of homeless men
Who squat in blankets looking morose
Around a lickless fire,
*

Paltry from lack of oxygen
Or lack of fuel, or lack of hope.
They have developed the morose look
Through dint of unbearable lives
And a need to beg effectively.
They believe that looking miserable
Will bring in extra income,
But their crafty sub-expressions
Convey their ulterior selves
Who perhaps at one time were lucky
And had warm houses in the Hamptons
And perky wives who perhaps could cook.
What devils came and robbed them of
Everything like that, and left them
Like dried up husks of people
Telling depressing jokes to each other
As I bend to deliver the dollar.
The grime, the sad, the pathetic
Sticks to me as I straighten up.
I wear it down the street, ashamed,
As I feel their laughter land against my back,
Believing their derision and jealousy.
I wonder how to get out, how to get away
And know I made this too.
I have their emptiness in me.
It could be mine as well as anyone's.

THE MEXICANS

The Mexicans, walking in a crowd
With the overloaded grocery cart in their midst
Like a prisoner, all look the same
To someone who doesn't know the type.
Short to a man, and dark, with wide,
Open faces and intermittent silver teeth,
An easy way with the faces
When they smile at me—
*

Something in me they recognize
And smile   All at once
Knowing something.

Still, I hold back my love for the species;
Don't talk their language to them on purpose
Because if they know I can
Then I will have to.
If they were sure about me
Then I would always have to be
A certain way.
If my yearning to be among them
Were revealed
Then I would have to be among them.

Why don't you go back to the Yucatan
Where you can walk alone?

So many of them walk together
In a group that invites no one—
But me—I am invited.

How can they laugh that easy?
They walk along with the high basket,
Like a single thing they move,
And my yearning to say—
"Come to my car with all that food.
Here, in the back—put it in."
(I practice the words.)
"I can drive you so easy
To where you go. I love your kind."
Is held back, knowing or fearing
A difference in the kind
Who choose to come here
From that superior poverty
To work in demeaning ways
In the violence—la *violencia*
La *violencia de aquí* . . .
I hate the tourists who made you want
El *Norte, El Norte terrible*
Que *lo se querían tanto*—
*

Wanted it enough to leave
The superior poorness,
The red warmth,
Families who kept you, babies, wives,
To come here and walk the basket
To your man-smelling cramped home,
Sending back the checks to those others,
But living in the paradox
Of loneliness among your myriad fellows,
And losing the innocence of your people
In it too.

I linger in the parking lot beside the car
Watching your amoeba path up the alley,
Knowing I can never give you anything at all—
The secret love of a once-shared caste
Choked and silenced by the conventions of fear.

Liselotte Erlanger-Glozer

EVENING IN THE GARDEN
FROM *Poems in a Garden*

So falls the evening
shuttering down
gentian, crimson poppies, autumn crocus
for business
of bumblebee and butterfly.

The latest hummingbird
inspects the foxglove
once again
before it whirrs into
invisibility.

Soon moths
will sever themselves
from bark and sun-warm walls
searching for
sweet smelling ladies of the night:
evening primrose, stock
and heliotrope
the odor of vanilla
and Victorian sex.

PALLADIAN VICENZA
FROM *Places*

When I turned
into the piazza
the twentieth century
emptied itself
handed Vicenza back
to the sixteenth.

Pigeons fluttered
into the past
past glory
past memory
passed from everyday
to become nervous sculptures
on roof lines
meant to bedazzle
with order and symmetry.

Waiters
setting tables
flicked napkins
to whisk me
like graceless magicians
into my place
in time.

POPPIES (*Papaver Rhoeas*)
FROM *Poems in a Garden*

How hurriedly the poppy
moves toward the instant
of shining

How the husk breaks, reveals
blackness at the center. How
the faintest current of air
—a morning breeze—
releases the stamen's golden powder

Beauty makes way
for the extravagance of fruiting
the seed pod, many chambered
will release
into air, into soil

minute prescience
of next year's joy.

THE SUICIDE

When sunsets slipped from her hands
and her eyes disclaimed the perfection of roses
she still watched the wind as it groomed
grasses in patterns of color.

Those she had birthed and nurtured
built walls that excluded
and the voices of friends grew faint
over the alarms of her heart.

At the end her comfort
her refuge were pills
tiny paving stones on the road
to nowhere and nothing.

TIME CHANGES ALL

Time changes all:
The children, on life rafts of their making
float away
make you the curator
of the museum of their childhood
which they revisit
from time to time
bemused by so much past.

All changes in time:
days shrink   into themselves
while nights expand
turning the spotlight
on musty transgressions
rarely
on long ago joys.

Kate White

CAT-WOMAN REHABILITATED

Cat-woman stalked the streets
with thirteen meows on strings.
Through the P.O. window
they watched her with sideways eyes
stretch her tit
up through the collar
of her human shirt
and dig out fleas.
She squatted on the sidewalk
and buried her shit
in flower beds
with her hind legs.
She wasn't enough human
with dark blue magic
marker whiskers fanning
from the corners of the mouth
across the face so they banned her
from markets and bookstores.
When her pupils elongated
and grew tips
they scooped her up
and cleaned her up
and now she mops up
people's leavings
at the Good Sleep Motel.
At home in her trailer across the bridge
she's on the edges
but not the edge.
She's normal enough with two kitties,
Whiskers and Precious.
Her name is Lisa. People
are just beginning to know this.

A GOOD WAY TO LEAVE

Where
    redwoods
        waltzed
like rope swings in the wind
and holly leaves made a dragon's back
in the mulched alcove,
where
a pale yellow, beak-studded boa of goslings
circled a red Big Wheel
                parked
                    in the clover,
Sarah and I threaded over
and under the stretched
maroon necks of manzanita
tracking Donny Blue.

Days opened and closed in flame and petals.
Winter smoke
trailed silver tails
        over the shingles.
The moon
so drunk with gold
drowsed
grew listless.
At last his heavy
           lid
              closed
leaving us alone in a night
black as a camera's interior.
We left our rubber boots
        stuck like sentries
in the orange mud
and through the shutter click of a cricket's hiccup
we slipped out on socked feet and walked softly away
    quiet enough to let home
                stay sleeping.

INTERIOR DECORATING

I tried to pull an August madrone
into our kitchen:
latex cream on walls,
accents in a particular
coral-orange,
a border in those yellow silver spots
of decomposition.
I tried to create
a vision of the graceful aging
of a season.
That was when I believed
I could hold
what I loved.

I remember his presence
in other rooms
under his own incandescent sun
waiting for me
wanting from me
what moths want from light,
willing to burn.
That room
could never contain the volume
of my arrangement.

Now the creek has carried mountains
past that house.
Keys to unused locks
are lost.
I have since
painted everything white.

ABSOLUTION POEM

The apple tree planned all year
dispatching sap to her distant tips
conserving sunlight in her sheath of leaves.

She watched her sister fall with arms full
of green babies and watched her drop them
at the shock of earth and watched them scatter.

Through summer drought she rationed water
inflating petals, her most tender skin,
preparing for sons with godmother bees.

From pink ruffles she unfolded a brood of sturdy babies
kept their dull heads shaded
while her shoulders baked all afternoon.

At last she sent forth into the sun a barrage of apples
finely-formed sons, rosy, well-rounded
heads full of sugar and juice

and like young soldiers they fell
from their mother's extended arms
that said both stay and go.

So many sons! The ground was studded.
I couldn't walk without rolling their heads
peeling skin from their skulls.

As dusk began to gain on day
advancing its winter goal, I looked away.
Oh, I ate until I couldn't taste them

since I wasn't canning, cobblering, making pies
filling bushels for grateful people.
I was busy. I was lazy.

I passed her wasted effort daily, bruising.
So I'll tell how hard she tried, how high
were her green ambitions for the boys

and how their sunken orbs, brown,
infused with grass now feed her bodies
she'll give again, the Fall forgiven.

Julia Butterfly Hill

"OFFERINGS TO LUNA"

A tree
a life so many years gone by
history bound with each new ring and every scar
i lie nestled in Her arms
i listen to all She has to say
She speaks to me through my bare feet . . . my hands
She speaks to me on the wind . . . and in the rain
telling me stories born long before my time
Wisdom
as only Ancient Elders know
Truths
passed to me through Nature's perfect lips
She cries
Her overwhelming grief
sap that clings to me . . . to my soul
i wrap my arms around Her
offering the only solace that i know
giving myself as the only gift i have to give
a pitiful offering
to a Goddess such as this
but of myself
it is all that i have to give

Susan Maeder

LOVE DEMANDS

There is no arrangement to love,
no orderly tableau, not even
a moment of stasis where we
can stop and breathe.

Keep moving, love demands,
and nudges us up from our
cushions, out from under
our featherbeds, into the

waiting world. A pileated
woodpecker stands aslant
our favorite tree, needing to be
seen. A gray squirrel is loose in

the foliage. The grass has
greened into sight while
we slept. Brambles abound.
Even an early jasmine winks

and something glistens over
there, a rogue beetle in
its patent leather case.
Nothing fits particularly,

this belonging next to
that. No tree is wed to
sky or web to bush. No
crocus needs the brown crust

of earth it's broken through.
That crooked watering can
with its ring of rust is
unconcerned with the shadow

it casts. What purpose to the
peeling garden hose that bellies
its way toward the apple tree?
It is up to us to make

connections, to see how the
twig loves the tree, the bud
the twig, the unborn bloom the
bud, and from there we'll learn

the rest: the snake in the
tree, it's hiss, and then the
snap of the apple bitten, the
tales we invent to put sense

to what won't stop dancing.
Love says: go! reach! live!
and then hoists the sun up
into day. It only wants our

Full Attention. That's why it
tugs at our blood the way it
does, making its circles
inside us.

Listen. It won't give up.
Only turn your head on the
pillow. Look: something is
reddening outside the window,

something else is growing ripe.
The sky is lending us its light.
Hurry, love says, hurry.
Love says: hurry.

WHAT WE NEED

Put me in the lab.
There in my tucked white
I will become

an indifferent eye.
I am the one bent
to the scope, intent

on each ravenous
cell, inspecting its
journey out of itself,

its pluraling with the ease
of a knit-one-purl-two
precision.

I see radiant flowers,
their bud-life shattered,
their green wings blown full.

I see moon-flowers,
forever waxing, embracing
the stars, bringing

them home, bringing
everything home.

I am white,
in my lab, spying,
bent to the truth,

splicing realities,
watching the gods grow
beyond their old hearths

while we within
wither, our dreams
growing small.

We tend tiny fires,
having forgotten sun

and moon

having lost track
of magnanimous gods,
their splendid trajectories.

Something gray
has descended,
something

with no regard for
glory. Something
like ashes.

I can see it
around the edges,
fine as lace.

It looks benign.
It wants to love us.
It wants to teach us

something. At the far
end of my tunnel,
a membrane of light.

Gray. I can see gray,
and how gently
it surrounds us

defining what we need,
showing us everything
we need.

JASMINE

do you believe
in nature's dark mercy
where nothing shows

or are you tied
to her tangled abundance
greedy for the weave and web

of her green threads
all promise apparent

it's so easy to love
that star-flowered girth
everything in us rises

everything rises

but think of that
black place underneath
that upside-down heaven

black seeds in their place
and silent all that
opulence compressed

can you trust those gods ·
with their dark jobs

can you wait
and be still
while the world breathes

and nothing happens?

IF THE TREES SAY YES

If we are to survive
our ordered days that now,
bereft of shadowy substance,
stand exposed to every element:
raking wind

And fire of the cruelest kind
that has no rising, cannot climb,
but serpents in its agitation
feeding on the felled debris,

Then we must look to
a deeper place for resolution.
We have denied our gods, said No,
and chosen our cellular reality
over theirs,

Forgetting that our own red sap
rises, seasonal, bent on
the breathing in, then feeding back,
the perfect circle of intent
that we have learned from them.

We shall have to listen
as the rasping wind searches out
the corners where we hide, scouring
every angle of our too-bright days

And wonder each time we recall
the crack and thunder of their falling
if the trees said: Yes, we are done
and gave thanks to every creature
as they fell.

What have they left us then?
This gift of night, this final shadow?
If our days are stunned with light,
is this the place for our dark praising?
Is this the home of our new sight?

WHITE SONG II

The white nuns slip through the door
to touch her, strapped and muted,
on the table. How they must

envy her her belly, the thrumming
beneath the taut skin rendering her
monstrous, huge as the moon gone mad.

One wants to touch the mound with her
cool smooth palm; another to reach
inside and finger the impossible door,

passable only from the other side,
to measure and manipulate. Another
tends to the clank and clink in the

corner, silver symphony. What
do they want? Are they waiting,
yearning for the blood time, the

wild gush, the unstoppable, the
part where you nearly die, the
consequence? Are they proud,

joined at the hip in their whispery
sisterhood, all purity and penance?
Could they conceive of the night's

white passion, tented sheets all
blustery, this wanting that wed the
two brief dabs and led her finally

here? One flutters to her side
at the groaning, another gurgles
comfort from the other side.

A third, the youngest, has closed
her eyes. The white walls ghost
her. She disappears to white.

She is dreaming: a funneling,
a mewing, and then a silvering
into light. Here, here is the

corded gift, slippery as sin,
the long blue length of him,
like silk, the heavy head.

She wraps and wraps him, white
and white, and wraps, and runs
and dreams her dreaming.

But looking down she sees her
red shoes flying, ribbons streaming,
red shoes are leaping, dancing.

Her blind red shoes are leaving
scarlet footprints in the night.

WHY NOW THE RIVER

FOR MY FATHER

Wish it would snow, but it won't,
given the light, given the stark glow
and the clattery trees. Moon's like a blister,
so sore. You sing in your sleep,

Small song like a coin tucked somewhere safe,
silly doo-wah, yesterday's fare. You're off-key.
Makes me laugh.

Why should it hurt to hear
stars crackling up there in the void?

Has nothing to do with you, pillowed,
your mouth-slot shaping the tune,
me watching your eyes roam, their quick,
shuttered beat tracing some other song,

Other night, some other blistery moon,
nothing to do with me.

Why now the road's white line rising
behind my own lids? It's not enough to be
here tracking you back and back?

Why now the river, riding the riverbank
steady as home, moon like a bone
in the black this time?

You're leaning too far to that other side
where darker, the days thin and thin,
who knows how cold, who knows how long
or how far.

Look out the window.
Old moon finally popped.
It's oozing a shine, an icy patina.
I'd be a fool to see snow where there is none,

But oh, for a snowman to bunch with my mittens,
punch eyes in with pebbles, twig hair,
give him pipe, tall hat and a broom.
Give him a song.

Lie back, lie back. True winter is here,
grown into the trees and the ground,
grown into the static gray river, erratic
weeds stiffened and sharp. No need to press on.

You're humming, remembering the whiskey times,
sweet bends in the river, the good thrum and flow.
Well, go. Span the muddy Ohio, sing Mississippi,
never missing an "s" or a "p."

Dark's folding in. The day's in eclipse,
a photographer's dream.
When the snow finally comes
how real will it be, how black?

DANGER

FOR JEANNIE V.

he wants to know
about me and bikes
and do I like that
buzz they say
gets girls off

oh boy, I think,
oh boy, I'll tell you
about j. and how she
shaved her head for
Halloween, going out
as mr. kleen to spook
the stuffy neighbors

how it took her seven
minutes   she told me:
I don't ever want to
know who's looking
in the mirror

then she bought a
bike, thick-wheeled
black and loud
I hated it

she made me ride it
stuck me on the back
behind her
grab me here like this
she said, fixing
my arms

like she's a boy
and I'm the girl
we're off

I stop being afraid
and learn the leaning
thing, how you sway
into the curves

the road strung out
ahead, behind
and now we're tough
       we're punks
       back off!

this thing between us
underneath us
loud as sex

we grind down, flying
me finding my hands
have found her hips

I'm holding her like
she's some stone man
pumping fire, everything

whizzing by
and now I know
there's no difference

that's what I find out
we're all stone in the wind
every curve is us

I'm the thrust and buzz
and yeh I've been
ready for this all my life

I open my mouth to her
when she turns around
our tongues do a little dance

then she's mr. kleen again
the wind is gone

that same year
I took a bus
across the states
watched it all slide by
through glass

I saw it all
but I don't know it

we rode so high and slow
engine tame as a pet
the cornfields
didn't interest me

my hands were resting
on my lap like birds
the driver coughed and coughed

the trip took days
and nights and days
a thousand times as long

as j. becoming mr. kleen
a few quick swipes
and she was new

I'll ride with you
I'll hold you there
feel it all
I'm not afraid

I've sailed with mr. kleen
across this concrete
continent   it was sweet

we never made it
to the other side

but you and I?
I can taste the wind
I can feel the morning
gravel making way

we'll roar into the day
the sun can't stop us

and when you turn
to me, the wind
fixing us against the sky

I'll open to you too
and this time
we'll keep dancing

Kay Lieberknecht

JOHN DEERE CATERPILLAR

I am a country woman,
  town worker;
So I'm a worshipper of
  yellow metal
  and rock.
Some people hang
  crosses over their
  beds and tables;
Sign of death,
  persecution,
  somehow hope.
I have two yellow metal models
  and a rock by my bed;
Signs of access,
  freedom,
  power.
Ever seen yellow metal at work?
  Jaws drooling rock,
  huge blades delicately
  buttering a country road.
Once I lived without land.
  I prayed for a boulder
  for my birthday
  and a yard to put it in.
I forgot to say which birthday,
  so I got yards and acres
  with boulders aplenty,
  just a few years later.

LIFE BEFORE WORK

I ease your gallop at the crest of the hill
To honor the descent of the moon.
A mountain, pregnant with pines,
Rests belly-up in the fog.
The gifts of this ride, like morning dew,
Will steam from my soul in the sun.

TO SPIRIT

Barely certain I can ride this wind,
I sink my pelvis deep behind your withers.
Gradually your jagged gait smooths.
Your back softens to my heavy thighs.
Wild power presses up into weight settling down.

My heart floats.

GENTLE AND STRONG

Gentle you came to my senses
        Like a star in the morning
        Like lemon in water
        Like mint on a pathway
        Like the breath of a horse
        Like the call of a quail
Strong you came to my senses
        Like the arc of a willow
        Like the burst seed of fennel
        Like dark dampened earth
        Like the swell of a wave
        Like wind through a cave
You came to my senses
I came to my own
I'm awake I am here with you
Gentle and strong

WITHIN—A STORM

Above the crackling protestations of my skin,
I can hear the murmuring of your hands.
You are cradling the wind,
Pulling the stars down close.
Your touch is the cooing of birds
When the rain is light.

IN LOVE

Sometimes when I pick my way through mud
To do my mundane chores,
My eyes slip up,
My arms stretch wide and high, and
I can't help but groan, and yell and
Laugh, in love with this clumsy,
Unbound land which loves me
Beautiful and stubborn.

PAIN

These days of pain
You must be brilliant to lighten me.
So you give me
>   Grasses stampeding before the wind,
>   A sliver of moon decorating thin lace clouds,
>   Flurries of sun and rain as Summer and Winter vie for Spring's favor.
My pain please take in laughter,
Bursting out,
Leaving me quiet in a hum,
Glad to be alive.

SISTER

Wide eyes,
Bright eyes,
Without sight eyes.

Sister in pain,
Sister in loss,
Sister in wishing without hope.

Sister, when you
Come to understand,
Let me soothe the aching of the light.

I was blind once too.

Ojos anchos,
Ojos claros,
Ojos sin vista.

Hermana en dolor,
Hermana en pérdida,
Hermana en deseos sin esperanza.

Hermana, cuando
Llegas a comprender,
Deja que yo calme el dolor a la luz.

Yo también estaba ciega una vez.

MOTHER

Aren't I a mother?
    Love those kids best when sleeping
    Listen to fickle food complaints
    Keep on cooking
Aren't I a mother?
    Tell stories of mom-as-kid
    Retrospective competition for clumsiest kid on earth
    Cheerlead for talking back to bullies
Aren't I a mother?
    Think up tasks and disciplines
    Agree on contracts and limits
    Relax those rules more often than not
Aren't I a mother?
    Take two weeks to get hold of the Tooth Fairy
    Put time, places and transportation together like puzzles
    Stroke a head hold a foot reading books
Aren't I a mother?
    Give name to a baby never born live
    Give thanks to a child lived too short
    Give how when what I can
Aren't I a mother?
    Hands and heart open
    To cradle
    And let go

Cynthia Frank

PANTOUM

the planet rocks
when we only believe in secrets
we are the key
turning endlessly in the dark

when we only believe in secrets
who knows the damage we do
turning endlessly in the dark
geographers without hope

who knows the damage we do
something whole drifts into a diagram
geographers without hope
confuse the map with the territory

something whole drifts into a diagram
I lose myself unbraiding your tangled hair
confuse the map with the territory
try to turn away

I lose myself unbraiding your tangled hair
we stumble across open pastures
try to turn away
find the fences before lightning strikes

we stumble across open pastures
mushrooms shoulder their way through the straw
find the fences before lightning strikes
under our cold toes

mushrooms shoulder their way through the straw
redolent and plump
under our cold toes
the secret territory stretches out

redolent and plump
your hair is full of dreams

✲

the secret territory stretches out
as you shake your head

your hair is full of dreams
the stars make tiny sounds like broken glass
as you shake your head
no secrets, you whisper

the stars make tiny sounds, like broken glass
the ground beneath us disappears
no secrets, you whisper
crickets call to each other in the dark grass

the ground beneath us disappears
like a blue sky, it's never a simple thing
crickets call to each other in the dark grass
to tell the truth

like a blue sky, it's never a simple thing
to know the price of a secret
to tell the truth
when we promise you safety

to know the price of a secret
could be your dreams
when we promise you safety
without wisdom, only hope

could be your dreams
we are the key
without wisdom, only hope
the planet rocks

LAKE OHRID

MACEDONIA, AUGUST 1988

a short walk from Slave Bakrachevski's house
down narrow twisting uneven streets
across the polished angular flagstones of the main square
the early morning roses are strong in the biting haze

a crowd of small skiffs, oars shipped,
bumps quietly against the stone dock
their blue, green, white, fuchsia hulls
strong against water the color of wet slate

men fish and tease each other quietly
their voices ripple out
and come back to them disguised as birds
water splashes under the flagstones

spills abruptly from second floor apartment windows
is sucked up by the hungry earth beyond the restaurant terrace
Albanian mountains push darkly through the mist across the lake
indistinct, threatening

two swans preen as they paddle slowly past the small boats
their lovely necks reflected suddenly in the lake
as the haze lifts
I'm surprised to see them
the lake is so vast, like an ocean

it is seven am
when a small rust-colored dog finds me and says, "Play!"
he dashes in front, turns to pounce on my shoes,
lags behind to shit authoritatively on a stone
then skips and scurries under the bumper of a passing car

when I arrive at my favorite stone bench
beside its low lichen-covered wall
the brazier is already lit in the church courtyard
the souvenir woman, round shouldered
and dressed in black as always
leans on her elbow behind the glass

the old church is almost hidden by bunches of fat green grapes
hanging from an old arbor
juice from the heavy splitting fruit drips slowly
onto an ancient marble slab
the priest's mumble drifts out into the morning

suddenly, the dog bristles and growls, but it's just for show
a diplomat, he leaves the large gray cat alone
he looks up at me, astonished at all I've missed
and just when I think I've been paying attention

Sarah Flowers

OFFERINGS

Outside hay bales that corner the plot of grass
grow more tall blades
than the worked earth planted with seed.
I pull strands of hair from a plastic brush.
They float off on the south wind.
Fingers of pines cast them on their needles.
Birds find them, twine one and then another
with moss, with redwood bark fibers.
I become a nest,
something sung to like sunshine and territories.

Every morning a robin is the dawn's voice
filling his chest with praise for spring, for home.
Each note encloses the woods, the meadows
the lignin-loving mushroom, down-side on a rotten log
rising phototropic, spores dehisced far beyond earth.

DIGGING THISTLES

Green fields turn brown
and sunlight holds me
with warmth that accelerates
an engine in my chest.
Log trucks run arteries
along the arms of summer
August breathing down my collar
and the growl of a jake-brake.

At noon I taste salt
mixed with dust.
In the woods beyond the meadow
a Hermit Thrush sings
variations of flutes
a timeless harmony
of earth under my fingernails.

A SOLITARY HARMONY

Alone the Hermit Thrush sings in two voices.
Silver flutes brocade the sound
clear and sad.
Still the morning star
lights dark unseeing dawn.

Each March brings a loss
an absence as of leaves in winter
and song laments one's solitary harmony.
Something sad in spring
is sad against the green
tips of vine and bush and tree.
New grass grows hollow instruments
and brightest sun makes deepest shade.

Continuing through the throat of June
sweet duality
the Hermit Thrush resounding self
twines strains
brief chrysalis and winged voice
across the space of time and universe
song's light shadow.

METAMORPHOSIS

Are we not pushed and pulled
into this life?
There are those spirits preferring
to remain unhoused
those who at birth cling
to their freedom
in a long embrace.
The small body
held by its feet, slack and empty.

Darkness is what she knows.
She is the universe
and we ask her to be earth.
For some the decision is slowly made.
We wait together in what seems to be
unending silence
while she hovers above her life
fascinated by its flame
finally giving oxygen to its fire.

Maluma Crone

SEIZURE

mind drifts gently out
like a small bird taking flight
I see it there afloat with
coffee table clutter before me
hovering amidst candy canes, clock, remote control.
I wait, watch its movement, wait.

mind drifts back, wings fluttering a moment,
settling where it belongs,
landed,
still now.

POST SEIZURES

I crouch, waiting, tentatively
in a corner in my body:
will it hold me again?
keep me safe?
can I come out now?
wrapping my spirit arms
around my fears
I slowly coax myself
back to trust:
first this breath,
then the next
slowly returning to the refuge
of one moment
built upon the next.

FEAR

my fear sits
in all her beauty
on the window sill
in the form of a feather

simple and there

Suddenly I treasure the light she brings me
    and, heart open,
instead of turning away,
    I meet her

so vibrant
    there for me to
    teach me all she knows.

Liz Haapanen

SOLICITING YES

This is the card of mystery
the challenger of fate
a vague and patient memory
nestled in the heart.

This is the gypsy death
the wormhole takeover
the time warp mind wobble
polarity shift far past midnight.

This is the time of crying, of crisis
and reprisal and of keeping boredom
at bay—just over the cliff of the next
deadline.

This is where we are:
Center stage and glowing
against the screen, fingering keys
touching down on dreams.

This is how it's been,
how it's going,
how it may be,
and so I urge
you to say
Yes, quickly.

MY MOTHER'S SORROW

I am not my mother's sorrow
or the tracks of her tears
now forming unnatural
furrows after years of
erosion—or the quickly
*

gestured shrug—too soon
erupting in defense, over
helplessness.

No, I will not welcome her
nor be her willing accomplice
from church to grave, dressing
room to skillet as she whispers
shame into my ears. She will not
accompany me to my lover's bed
to lay down the endless law of
disapproval.

And yet, she creeps
late in the velvety shadows
of darkness, gathering evidence
of sins committed. Unbidden
coach warning of damage done
she sees my body as godless
carnage for the vultures.
She comes with her luggage in tow
dragging picture frames with hard
memories just waiting to happen.

MORNING SONG

Like the morning glories in the field
common as weeds, however lovely
radiating their potent messages back to the sky
something forgotten suddenly blooms in your memory
and the snow thaws around your heart
and the world becomes alive in you
as you rise up in your meadow and shine
with color and fragrance and movement
of the grasses whispering shushes
and the frogs wake up the day
calling your name, Renée, Renée, Renée . . .

(Written to a sister recovering from a failed suicide attempt.)

Joan Stanford

RETURN

Leaving the main road . . .
　　Entering the twisted path
　　　　slowing way down.

I park . . .
　　I move into the dark . . .
Small among towering trees.

I step on stones
each one leading me closer to the door
with its scribed instruction.

I enter
the sacred circle.
I enter my
sacred center.

From here we share
our deepest selves,
trust intimacy is possible,
Blessing the dark, the light,
the movement, the pauses,
the space between, as the space within
Allowing, inviting, celebrating.

For Marilyn's group October 9, 1997.

CARE AND CLEANING INSTRUCTIONS (AFFIXED TO THE LABEL ON THE HEART)

To remove pain stains from a broken heart,
 (works also for those stubborn, hard-to-remove stains left from shattered dreams)
  Soak in tears.
Not just overnight, but for years.
Let stand.
Do not rub, scrub or agitate.
  Wait.
Time and tears will do the job.

Place on windowsill.
Let sun and moon watch over,
 (teach of cycles)
Expose to soft, cool breezes
whose touch, felt but unseen,
speaks in heart's tongue.

After some time
place heart in dark woods,
  in a sunny meadow,
   often by the riverbank or seashore,
 (the flowing on, the next wave, teach of healing)

Burn a candle, sage.
 Sing a lullaby.

To test for doneness,
take heart to where children play,
  a spring garden,
  near new lovers.

Wash on gentle cycle,
 (a circle of women works wonders!)
Dry, low heat, delicate.
Wear on sleeve.
Repeat as needed.

Jane Reichhold

LIVE DANCING

his shyness asked
I had never danced before
with a woman
his breasts slightly smaller
than mine touching mine

knotted
his biceps pressed me against
the lace of his gown
low-cut and revealing
a few dark chest hairs

pointed
the toes of our high heels
slid together
in the space between my legs
a swelling in two sizes

musk
sweetened sweat slipped
between us
shapes rose and blue
in the hot jazz riffs

dizzy without breath
time rolled into one
past life
we have been together before
now male; now female

OPENING COLORS

opening colors
the air that brings back
the swallows

he touches the wing
before boarding the plane

airport insurance
beside the machine he peddles
religious relics

in the most sacred place
two figures twined together

temple moon-viewing
negative publicity
makes it exciting

chills on the autumn beach
ghost crabs scuttle for cover

singing
the roof holds up
the rain

in the locked trunk
mildew everywhere

her wrinkled face
someone slept there but
left in a hurry

wailing in grief
she thinks of herself

river's mouth
where salt mixes with freshwater
a mulatto child

the shell game played
with buttons and raisins

full-moon breakfast
shining on the plate
    glazed donuts

    first day of camping out
    the sweets are eaten first

light
inside a cage of ribs
    a healthy heart

    his donation to the college
    bought more poetry books

discovery
of the unexpected
    flower

    he had no idea
    she was still a virgin

spring planting
the farmer family postpones
    the wedding

    a seedling stretches light
    underground white roots

genetically
the tomato engineered
    by accident

    in anger he loses his cool
    tears the envelope jagged

ice breaking up
something in the creek
    wants out

    the snowman bows
    loses his head

new school
the smartest girl
　　　is also the prettiest

　　　playing with her dolls
　　　the child molester grins

change the laws
one conviction for rape—
　　　the death penalty

　　　given a pomegranate
　　　her wish—with its days

what makes the moon shine?
it's the home of every bad
　　　poem written

　　　the dead watch us
　　　how we spend ourselves

hours—minutes
the flimsy veil that ties us
　　　to this blue-green ball

　　　killing time with video games
　　　kids wait to grow up

an old story
dust it off to read again
　　　Huckleberry Finn

　　　paint on the iron fence
　　　blisters and peels

thin membrane
such as would red
　　　be poppies

　　　bowl of several stones
　　　to the south seven doors

DRESSED TO KILL

We are God's clothes; without us God cannot be seen.
We are the diapers when the soul is new; egotistical and raw.

We are the pacifiers, nipples and teats that soothe
The hours growing smooth tight; reason and inquisition.

Our lives are the little soap operas to fill the boredom
Between earthquakes, hurricanes and another year.

Our songs of praise and thanksgiving grate on God's ear.
Patient as parents at the piano recital of the privileged.

Our churches and holy buildings are blots that blemish
The better regulated realms of renewable nature.

Like a clothes closet run amok, we philosophize,
Iron the ruffles and pad the bras of being.

LIGHT MOON

Going to view the moon I find
it clouded over and the sky on earth

looking inside myself the moon shines
regular as a barren woman bleeds

when flowing freely and very full
moonlight is added to my own light

makes me a bit more crazy and I join
the moonlight bounding up from every surface.

As I move moonlight dances in
moonlight and the vibrating becomes incredible.

The gate opened and meadow moonlight
flowed down the road moonlight where crows

found grass moonlight to be tasty
but the road moonlight is easier to walk on.

Sometimes car moonlight takes precedence
but when it is gone moonlight refills the space

in every face are the long white columns
from eye to sky of moonlight realized

the question of moonlight is answered moonlight
even the open mouths of the dead are filled with it.

What seems lost one night is discovered earlier
in another place that is yet to be moonlight

DAY WOMB

a nail upon a wall
        a place to hang a note
only sun and rain write
        a bookmark for the days
I close the book of poems
        to find I am surrounded

stories trees tell each other
        echoing in the high winds
pressed into the form these words
        bark and leave, root to branch
out of such poems we build
        chairs we give our backs to

growing older the house
        moves its shadow on the porch
wind blows the sway of trees
        rough-sawn boards grow dark
it is just a phrase I know
        but it feels like the truth

PASSOVER

memory of fields
        in my mouth again
sun grown green
        and rain the fire
ripened into sacred wheat
        enters me as bread

why does the river stand
        obelisks of ice in spring?
as if all gravestones melted
        swift, silver and sustaining
memory grows into a wild iris
        that sucks on bees and sunshine

river of life they explain
        how we come and go
earth built of sunshine
        moved by the spin of stars
when we become incandescent
        water leaves us like an angel

CANDLES WITH CAKE

spring snow drove her
        in a rented car
her birthday and his
        on one blue lake
gamblers winked to grin
        mother and son still joined

snake oil and rust
        the high price of trust
hope and health from the things
        risen with healing in their wings
✻

thus centered in truth lies
    pills and salves of daily foods

as the seed bends a tendril
    last oblation to the earth
raising my hands splayed
    as two green leaves
fantasy you sneer?
    no, I've just eaten bread

Robin Rule

Excerpts from DOGS OF POMPEI

II

Dogs drive me deep
into the dark intricacies
of Etruscan maze.
Sharp teeth shepherd my naked calves,
drive me to that place
just before coming
where the body aches.
As I give up my will
and stumble downward,
I am a long, wanton vowel.

Deeper they herd me down dark corridors
dedicated to lust; my hips
sway in the dead air, mingling new music
with the groans of ghost women.

A doorway breaks the labyrinth wall.
Pale streaks of light from broken roof
reveal the leather-skinned skeleton
of a delicate-boned temple whore:
now curled in volcanic ash,
now etched indelible in petite mort.

For hours I gaze at her sleep with envy.
I turn to ask of the dogs: *what is my place in all this?*
and find I am alone: the light fading
and no map to the gates of the city
now closing with the distant clang of metal.

I lie down in the temple,
wrapping my arms around her shoulders,
nestling my face into her angel wings.
In broken memory, I dream ashes
and the levels of fire. I dream the once buried
and now uncovered stories.

III

Under the olive trees, I lay with the ghosts of gods.
Ripe berries, hot in sun, fell on my naked thighs.
I rode the earth with undulating hips,
my wine-sweet, dark-bread   sex
pushing into the fields.

I breathed out the names
of all the lovers who have heaved beneath me
like volcanos. As I called out syllables,
the ghosts fingered me
with temple touch and songs of feast.
I made the sounds of Vesuvio pushing
heat through dark tunnels with your name.
I spoke in tongues long before Jesus,
long before Babel was built.

IV

In the last years of Pompei, one man worked
advertising, when before there were many.
He painted the house walls with vermilion
graffiti announcing actors coming to town,
houses for rent, stolen goods, politicos
and a secret symbol for the sweet girl he lay with
on pay-days at the temple of Venus.
Every week, a new message, like newspapers
in small towns, but always the same love-brush
stroking her curves into an unpronounceable name.
In the end, when the fire and ash came,
he left a mystery for archeologists:
which curled charred body in the bathhouse
once curved delicious around the heart of an artist.

V

Staring at Michaelangelo's Moses,
my ears are smashed by the cacophony
coming from the street below this small church.
I wander down to the stone bridge separating
me from thousands of women marching
against Amato, the prime minister.
—*La nostra disponibilita e finita*—
—*Siamo stufe di essere discrimiate*—
Amato: non far conto 'sulle' donne—
Huge banners splashed with words
and the large oak tree of the Partito Della Sinistra
are carried by many women and girls and old stregas
who are singing, laughing and demanding
the whole city listen to them as they tell us,
Our willingness is finished—
We are fed up with being discriminated against—
Amato, the women will not be there
as he proposes to cut work hours and health benefits
in a country where women are told to have children
until they die in childbirth.

I am waving to upturned faces. I have forgotten Moses
until I see the faces of the polizia, cold as the stone I lean over.

VI

This glass I hold in Apollo's house
mirrors my hand carrying lipstick to my mouth.
This art is a mirror of a lost world: even though
the sensuous ritual of dark split cherries
is now Chanel and glossy magazines.
Where once I was dressed in prehistoric shadows,
now I am clothed in alphabetic t-shirt
I discard for the gods, leaving only my lips arrayed
in summer's memory. My camera rests on Apollo's feet;
his blank eyes, lenses which open on sunlight: the kiss.

VII

My face is veiled like any good joy-daughter
in the Temple of Pan. I wait for you
in a small pool of water, draping myself
over the small bronze form of his body.
You could do anything to me right now.
You could spread and enter
this American object of desire, if
you wanted me like I want you. I wait.
The camera shutters: my hips thrust and want.
This moment of olive oil and red wine
is eternal. I am   *Everywoman*
waiting for the Everyman   promised in
our childhood dreams of bride's veil white and shoes:
the photo book: swollen with desire.

VIII

I fell into the aqueduct and crawled
up river into the barking of dogs.
Motorcycle boots, cobblestones: it's all
too much opera as I stumble onto
marble like some temple-singer waiting
for the beginning notes to an aria
I don't know the words to yet. I'm breathless
waiting for the libretto, like I'm waiting for
just the right god to tell me it's okay
to stay up late nights at the typewriter
in summer, in my underwear, in hope of
finding just the right word to describe
the hot dark mystery of loving.
Outside the window: begging dogs.

Janet DeBar

LUNCHEON IN MARIN

Young women tempt old men.
They lean forward, those girls in tight blouses
and softly speak: chocolate,
raspberries, pears poached in brandy.

Young men tempt the certain-aged women.
They lean forward, those boys in black aprons
inviting, inquiring whether she'll have the
chocolate, raspberries, pears poached in brandy.

Foods are intoned like sins, like sins
we know we will commit and from which
these waiters already grant our craved indulgence.

We know many are starving.
It's the old story.
Many have always starved
and will always starve
until either the two-legged race dies out
or suffers a major revelation.
Every driver struck dumb on the Damascus freeway

But here, today, in Marin, we pay to be tempted
To hear potential sin recited like Shakespeare.

And it is sin. We sweat it, we stew in it,
we chew, we swallow. How easily it slides down:
chocolate, raspberries, pears poached in eau de vie,
in water-of-life; in brandy.

NAUDHIZ

Naudhiz is the tenth rune signifying need or distress with the esoteric meaning of need-fire and deliverance from distress.

That time of year
when I rock in my grandfather's chair
and stare unblinking at the fire
a cliché; so many have done it before.

This time last year
I was neither here nor there
when I rocked, when I rocked
to the rhythm of crackling logs.

Need-fire on the hearth
kindled from friction
hisses the story, spits the old passion.
I was ashes: now I am stone.

These elementals, stark
lack sophistication
lack precise rendering derived from a schooled perception
They are simply there
What place have they here
in these times when bare earth's hidden?

Many great houses have fallen
Many men have died
Many women have unloosed storms from their hair
and rocked in their grandfathers' chairs
and dreamed of turning water to wine.

How many permutations
when the five consider four?
Suck bitter root from the cellar
and taste how sweet is the lord:
The suavity of sweat, the salinity of blood—
My tongue rejoices in savories.

Grace gives grace too easily,
Tap-hammer knee with reverence
*

and jerk response
I say cross out all houseled words.

Unstone churches, dismember
the architecture of man
Let giant boulders ring high places.

The Chartres floor maze—
can any remember its original dance?

That time of year
when we'd coax back the sun
from sea-deep grave
to our toil-bleared farms.
Wheels burn within wheels:
The bone bubble glows
as its weight sinks my neck
beneath a lighted globe.

BLANKSTONE

(Being the first and last page of the procrastinator's journal)

She always meant to get her thoughts together
just as she always meant to do dishes after dinner
but was so tired just having finished washing up lunch and breakfast
together
(you need a clear counter to prep that evening meal,
inevitable)
meal followed inevitable meal
and dust fell down like Jack and Jill.
Whatever she had to do, she hated and tried to avoid:
This habit eventually encompassed all action.
She tried to protect loved things from necessity.
Ordinary grace was denied her entirely
by whatever entity, her own self, or as the drunkards say,
a higher power, dispensed such favors.

Life slid by, a rough sledge pulled through country mud.
Wheels she'd exchanged for wooden runners.
Events became linear, stretching towards infinity,
time measured out in Occam's severed actual,
meaningless beyond each individual instance.

Between self-forced obedience to what she perceived as demanded
were the pure blank spaces.
These became harder and harder to leave.
She had formed an addiction to nothing—
to sitting and staring at fires
fixing on that focus
where
flame leaps free from black crystal.
Every thing else was intrusion.

Though what part of her sensed trespass
she could not say.
It felt almost physical.
Her body refused to get up,
each limb tied down like Gulliver's
by threads too fine to be discerned.
It was too much effort to go to another floor
and search for yesterday's undone work.

One evening toward the end of twilight
She finally collected herself enough
to sit down with paper, a pen
to consider why she had surrendered to emptiness
or if her surrender was indeed a rebellion
a refusal to yield to what she perceived as expected.

But nothing was ever expected.
Nobody expected anything.
She herself expected nothing.
She sat unblinking on an upper floor, the fire laid and unlighted.

MR. HAPPINESS

Monsieur Heureux was a purveyor of adornments who lured Madame Bovary into debt and ultimately suicide.

Monsieur Heureux, Mr. Happiness
He's shrunk these days from his 19th century fullness
Thin
as a piece of plastic that slips in your wallet

Thin, thin, thin
as the french letter in your pocket
you never bothered to read, let alone open

M. Heureux, Mr. Happiness

He's here for your instant gratification

and the price why it's a nothing in another tongue, a misery
not worth thinking about

One slight breath can lift
acid free tissue
which protects the obscured icon of desire
he's offering you.

Pray for this object which subjects you
Breathe out desire
Breath lifts thin tissue
revealing silk, marbleized
like the flesh of a prime animal

an interlacing, a tracery of white
pathways through blood.
(Who, wearing this fabric incarnadine
would not herself become an icon?)

It's almost as if a farm child had held out hands
beneath the inverted slaughtered creature
and printed her digits' whorls over fresh butcher paper
with the ink of the slit throat fountain—
a signature beyond denial

I've printed fallen leaves like that.

Breath stirs the leaves, breath lifts the tissue
Breathe for Monsieur Heureux, for Monster Happiness
His lungs wring out oxygen from your exhalation
Your sigh of desire brightens his blood
Whatever you acquire is in his interest
and it will never be enough

LADIES HOME JOURNAL

I stood with my arms full of unironed linen
placemats, runners, my mother's ancient tea towels
and thought
I should not submit myself to the iron:
these things have lain rumpled for months now.
Let them wait another day
Instead, write a poem.

I heard Sylvia crying in the kitchen.

Nobody wants to know the essence of worn fabric.

Up rose old yaller:
So many words exist already, so excellent, so many feelings
in ten-point type on onionskin
seventeen hundred twenty pages if you start
from Song of Myself and end with Kathy Song.
From Song to Song one thousand seven hundred twenty pages
and all the winnowed out, not chaff, surely.

Waters rise, trumpeting
of great beasts, sobbing of small
quick animals—you have forgotten us—as an anthology of arks
floats towards time's other shore
So many left, so many taken—
only the mind of god can know them.

And you there, tearing a grocery bag into scrap paper
too lazy or too violent to search out proper tools:
*

a stationary pad, a pen
making do with dull lead—
(She's crying over the burner)
and you dare whisper "My likeness, my sister"
(She's kneeling in front of the oven)
when you won't shake smooth that towel
which dried so many dishes
(She's blowing out the pilot)
when you won't look at the napkin which holds the impress
of her face.

Some things I have chosen not to examine
these threadbare rags I call towels, worn out long ago.
I cannot bear to throw them away
easier to iron them than to think about them
easier yet to leave them tumbled in the corner.

(Pay no attention to the odor. Keep all windows closed.)

Submit to the iron.

Zomala Abell

THE POEM I HEAR

The poem I hear this rainy morning
is wild
not responsive to my gentle query
nor to the familiar rustle of fresh pages
turning in my journal.
This morning
I don't want to wrest control from the torrent
or tame the words of desolation.
I want a lamp, a phone call
and cereal warm with nurturance now.
Outside my window
the growling whinny, snapping branches and shadow flashes
whirl in wetness.
The poem
as translucent as water
pounds down the soil, muddies my mind
and beats a persistent invitation
to wash clean of comfort.
With no warning
the rain stops.
As the wind waits
I find myself
still looking out the window
where in stillness
now
neither loss nor possibility
obscures my view of freedom.

ROOTBOUND

Spike leaves spike
talk bristle my caution
potted plant root tendrils
fifty years twining
You touched
the body that I was
She touched
the body that I was
I want everything back
that ever happened
minerals in the soil
growth in the stillness
and water
water to shine my green

UNTITLED

Almost touching hands
Almost nudging hips
We are comforted by the thin blanket of space between us
And the many sure days of time since our last kiss
We sit on the white couch
Our feet are on the straw mat of the floor
You are wrapped in echo memories
I am clothed in empty skin of loss
The gentle air is aching to embrace us
But it doesn't dare to touch
Such delicate cocoons of ash
The circulation in our feet
Is slowed by blame
The bones of our hands have been left
Paralyzed by struggle and desire
We sit in perfect discord
A salvo to the illusion of consummation, separation and despair
Neither of us can see
That the white walls of the room remain firm in witness to the truth
That this blessed love remains exalted and untouched.

CLEAR SKY

Suddenly, this soft blue afternoon
Strikes like lightning
In agonizing orgasm
I am blinked awake
To no image in the infinite mirror

Jane Harris Austin

DAUGHTER'S MEMORY BANK

standing alone
stranger behind
I touch mother's hands for the last time
a few sobs
a hand on my back, "appropriate empathy"

Oh, if only I could go back
embrace her
sob
loud
hard
for hours
bring life back to her
NO; bring her back to her body
to my body
to laugh and chat
have a cup of coffee and
linger a bit

FALL

like the eerie
still
spance
when twilight dawns
fall sinks in
quietly

shorter days
crisp shadows

new year beginning
for bright minds
and empty notebooks
my 60th school year

AJIJIC

we devoured the
orange, sweet
full

moon the first night
in Ajijic

from hotel patio
through cobblestone streets
black gates
brick arches
wrought iron stairs
to roof top

but ah . . .
you on the coast saw the same moon

it outshone the brilliant
fuchsia bougainvillea
peach hibiscus
red geraniums
orange and purple birds of paradise
all climbing toward it

last evening
the palate of flower colors
shone in the sunset and
reflected off the clouds
through the scent of star jasmine
and ah . . . hah
you on the coast
saw the same sunset

FOREVER UPON MOUNTAINS

I watch grandsons three and six and their mom
take off on chair lift up Werner Mountain
from where we stepped into gondola to ascend
for their parents' summer wedding ten years ago

Aleck rides with his mom, grinning wide, attached by a wee ski
Jasper wides alone, chest expanding, sitting proud
comes down that hill deftly plowing right into the gate
for the second run

These three I cradled in half my arm so short a time ago
tonight will allow a cuddle once more with a bedtime story
But, with six solo runs under his belt, for how long?
How long?
He grew a mountain today as the world watches
Olympians at Nagano

then we stand at the bottom of Howelsen Hill which has trained
so many medal winners
as the crop for 2010 is seeded

I retell a lesson told to me by one from Norway
who skied in those winter games long ago
his grandfather's first lesson to him at four
was how to fall
"To be great, one must know how to, must not fear,
the fall."

We share threads
weave new blankets
as the old unravels

ABUSIVE HOUSEHOLD

I rake through pictures and hear angry voices
I come to frozen stillness
wanting to hear and know what's going on
not wanting to know what's going on
want pictures to hold the memories of love
want memories
want silence
want love
want silence
want to know
want
out of want
pictures grow
and silence
and voice
for truth, and tomorrow and love

Kathy Watson

MAMA

I have been here before,
hollering in the pain
of childbirth.
Why are you
always leaving?
The birth process
repeats itself.
I scream.
You move from me,
farther each time.
What if I stood silent?
No tears
on my cheeks
Did not feel
the tides rush
in and out
of my body.
Would it be easier?

"Mama" I hear your voice
call me
and the pain
is good.

MY LOVER

His voice
soothes me
like the first
cool breeze
of summer
rustling the curtains
of an open window.

The places
on my body
where his hands
first touched
still burn
like glowing
embers
waiting for
the slightest stir
to set
them ablaze.

ON THE NOYO

Who sleeps now
in that room
where two souls
came together?
Flood gates lifted
and their bodies flowed
and mingled with the River,
tossed and turned with the currents
to finally settle in still
reflective pools.
Bare feet wore paths
across linoleum floors
through gardens
*

and under orchards
to places where we stretched naked in the sun.
In this fertile soil
we planted our future,
wept and laughed,
plowed and nurtured.
Through these twenty-seven years,
our bodies
have been wound together
so tight
that it seems
there is not
a place
where I end
and you begin.

Annie Correal

WET AND NAKED

You, with
eyes like sea anemones, turning inward, wet and naked
utterly benign, lured me to tear you from your rock,
causing me an old violence and a resolve to change
because you and boys like you, all messy,
wailed at me like high tide blisters pulsing from the kindness
of your supernatural hearts,
begging for a little war somewhere,
a little sweet streak of sadism,
a little Russian matriarch me, to save you from
dying skinny and unabused.
You wanted me like an injection of Ezra Pound
in your morning coffee because
it just didn't seem logical to love something
that strong, so early.

160 S. HAROLD STREET

Indiscretion was tattooed
all over our reputations,
but laughter was our grand entry
into the world of adolescent parties
and carnal knowledge,
a world, dragon sister,
that more closely resembled
us kneeling in a torrent of loose change
and cigarette butts, wilted flowers,
rain and crossword puzzles.

And your house was like a compass point,
a pole from which our days
emanated like sound.
Not like the sound of wind chimes,
✻

but with the strength of the mechanical climb
and the clickety-clack of
an irretrievable and tummy-turning
disposition toward disaster.
Birds of a feather
hear the current
of mischief
before it hits the frame of the
litany of everyday existence.
We were there to catch calamity in our
soft, young laps
and cradle it like a wounded
raven, blue-black,
unsavory and loud,
crumpled, shrieking
with the joy of the fall.

JUÁREZ

Because I always liked what was
fierce in the sensuous sphere,
I prefer a Bordertown holiday.
Juárez right before December.
Juárez smell of polvora dust.
Oh, ha ha Juárez cross the border
with a quarter, cross the river,
turn on a dime from civilized to cracked sidewalk.
El Puente Santafe over murky water hoisting beer cans
and tins of greasy ass beans right before sinking
down to Juárez. No more El Paso, without grass, oh
our flight, injured birds—let us be light with our wings
and our cares—let us fly south for the winter,
robbed blind of our nests and the rest is just
Juárez welcoming our nervous hands
and wide open feet and mouths that
taste third world, refried
Nudy Bar tequila with hallucinogenic worms
undulating their dead hips at the bottom of the canister
*

slip sliding, subdividing hope down the banister
of the Hotel Continental.
Landing soft on the peppermint green lobby tiles
me with a little flight-headed girl between my words and the world
of
Mexico.

Ballads like *el llanto me llega*
el juego del amor me juega
las lágrimas, ay, ay, ay,
saying when the weeping comes for me
the game of love it plays for me
the tears ay, ay, ay.
Another corona,
I'll loan you a peso
these marvelous days, oh
it wasn't so warm in Juárez.
We buried our hands deeper
in our pockets in Juárez
Where the buildings were built
Low enough to see America
On the four o'clock horizon,
Where the buildings were built low enough
To want to stay forever.
And our cheap room never stopped singing,
Humming with the pump-slump-pumping
of machinery all the way till bordertown
dawn.

Down by the market long lace cloths
running swooooosh . . .
wish . . . up in the greasy wind
and vendors pushing on us, the
yellow-haired.
Too much to bear,
another shot of treason
all the more reason to flee.
Coca Cola, ro-sham-bo-la,
home grown music
synthetic
*

Jukebox pump-slump-bumping us clear into
bordertown dawn dance floors
made of plywood
shoved into
the earth.

Pilgrim fathers, patriarchal brothers,
if I give thanks I'll give thanks
from the depths of my spicy throat,
tomato-slathed
margarita-salted lips,
and filthy little hands emerging like snails to the
bartender
and the money-lender.
Just the way Texas and Mexico kiss
right here before
me
like a gaudy threshold red tinsel
Prostitute Juárez,
dear black coffee
creamy accents of American meets
Espanol.
Yes, I'll Give Thanks for the flock of birds
like fugitives
or sprinkled pepper
stirred upward by the horns honking
Thank
You,
Thank
You,
honking
Mexican sun,
Runnin' Mexico,
plump-slump-Pumpin'
Mexico all over the taxi dashboards
with their stickers of
La Virgen.
Thank you Mexico
raw people
religion
*

and superstition
in a
pink and aquamarine
hologram.

I'll dye my hair black and
buy eyes to match the birds and
I'll swarm one-way
in pumps all fatuous
like an inverted fuchsia.
I'll slam my pallor to the table
like an empty shot glass and shatter
moderation with
the way hard alcohol does a fan dance
no-chance-fandango, melodramatics,
soap-opera-tango.
I'll let my head crack on the haphazard
concrete sky of Juárez,
selling my junk to the moon goddess
sipping swanky circles like
La Virgen,
nothing more than blind beggar
hallucinogenic worm laughing
up through the bottom of the
arteries

of

Mexico.

HOME FOR POOR CHILDREN DYING OF CANCER, BOGOTÁ, COLOMBIA

Teresa, like a tiny dove made of crayon, held a wing over her nose
so as not to smell her own body decaying. Death came with a call
like flickering sunlight shadowed through red wine, or blood
a word no one used there, as they flew down the hallways,
the altruistic ghosts,
the healthy led by conscience
✢

to be day in and day out
nervous, awaiting the latest
tiny church bell to be tapped
from the heights,
the white candle set to recede
unto itself in the chapel,
the name of the victim
scrawled on a yellow legal pad,
someone calling someone else and
the bedpan rid of the last greenish excrement
of a child deprived of life,
suddenly, in room 48.

And it was as such, this was not a hospital,
but a place for those who could not afford treatment.
It was a moratorium, and when I asked Teresa
what that meant she said
"it means stay until you stop staying."

I loved the windows there,
the sun on the white tile.
I watched a building grow
and another fall down for a whole year,
while they wept and wished
fervently to have been born blond, like me.
And blue in the way of the iris, and Teresa
told me she would have preferred to be born
with no brain and a pretty smile and a white dress
in which to stand before my favorite window
and dance with me, in English, she said.
Teresa was seven and black
and laughed far too ruefully
and taught me to name each night sky,
dutifully vomiting the blood before
she slept,
as to avoid choking in
her sleep.

And it was such, this place.
The shrug of God,
*

Home for the Blessed Forgotten.
We did not fight the muddled intrinsics of cells
that like an embarrassed blush,
spread from the bones to the tombs,
unobstructed, not detained from their destination unknown,
which was everywhere in the way only things unseen
can fester, everywhere there is to be
in the fallen limbs of infants.
Here Cancer and Poverty met.
Here they joined like lovers and killed.

And there we stood, the volunteers, like a bowl of daffodils in the windows,
obsolete, clean fish, tired, silent,
Queezy, wandering with the idiot smiles while a thousand jaundiced souls,
waited for our voices in the rough afternoon light, sliced
by the shadows into triangles of light,
sleeping mimes cut by the infiltrated
remnants of a backward society.
Here the children relinquished their
hold on life
while coloring little messages to their
parents. Promises compiled from the scraps of
the industrial glare,
downtown.
And we'd supply the crayons and mix Tang
cheerfully,
and wait for the sharp soprano voice
of the death bell from above,
and it would come,
and so we would speak a little
louder to drown it out.

All afternoon I would listen.
Two blocks away was the black market.
Emeralds were being passed between filthy hands
and only for a moment the brilliance of green,
the memory of a primordial jungle existence was
caught between the fingertip and the exchanged money,
and I listened hard. I listened to understand the falling
price on life.
*

I want to understand why I could look
these children in the eye.

Teresa told me true hunters must be strong enough to watch
the hunted creature die.
Teresa, like a tiny dove made of crayon, held a wing over her nose
so as not to smell her own body decaying. Death came with a call
like flickering sunlight shadowed through red wine, or blood.
Blood and phlegm, the guilt at the end,
sharp as a flame burning each of us out of our stone-cold sobriety.
O, vigilant destruction, you are the child who still holds my fingers
in sleep crying, "Guerra!" Crying war.

Jess River

UP A CREEK

She took
herself up
a creek
far up
beyond the end
of the trail
to a spot
so silent
she could hear
her thoughts
move
from one
to another
crossing
streams
rock by
smooth
or mossy
rock
log by
stump
she got
her feet
wet.

FOR JOHN (*After Carl Sandburg*)

The love of tall trees be for you.
Stand among sinuous roots, or sit;
feel patterned bark, let fragrance heal you.

The love of small stones be for you.
Stroll by heaving stormy sea,
let earth veins, colors, fill your pockets.

The love of solace be with you.
Sit at familiar formica counter,
exchange exquisite chit chat with waitress.

The love of old bookstores be with you.
Smell and feel of long-loved leather,
ancient wisdom neighborly with new.

The love of long rain be with you.
Tears we've waited to share
fall down around us, raincloak of healing grief.

The love of simple song be with you.
Unembarrassed, beyond performance,
in partnership with unassuming birds.

The love of small shrines be for you.
Statues adorned with tinsel and beads
turn aesthetics on her heavy head.

The love of home gardens be for you.
Splash of marigold, thrust of chard,
blush of blooming beauty everywhere exalted.

The love of small homes be for you.
Waking the sleeper within, opening hearts
to changes we must make for future's sake.

The love of great ferns be for you.
Lustily living in shade and damp,
embracing rotting duff as splendid succulence.

The love of dark earth be for you.
Holding in trust each tear, each silken earthworm,
weaving air and health round robust roots.

WHATEVER I EMBRACE, BECOMES

Space
inside my ribs
embrace

Space
inside my lungs
becomes

Space
inside my eyes
embrace

Space
inside

WHILE THE WIND OF THE MIND SWAYS THE STARS

A VILLANELLE FOR KARIN, AND FOR WHIT

The first "official attempt" to explain flying disks came from Japan, where a general on maneuvers saw "mysterious lights swinging and circling in the southern sky" throughout the night. Investigators ordered to determine what caused the strange occurrence, concurred, "it was only the wind, making the stars swing." The date: September 24, 1235.

While the wind of the mind sways the stars
and the rain of our grief reconciles us
our barque changes sails, turning homeward.

Thirteen white umbrellas are snapped up in vain
and a petulant soul finds no solace
while the wind of the mind sways the stars.

A covey of quail stretch their wings in the change
and importance rethinks itself, backwards, as
our barque changes sails, turning homeward.

Some things insignificant rise before eyes
used to measuring, counting, securing
while the wind of the mind sways the stars.

All our locked away longing arises in tune
and the drum of the world sounds the heartbeat, when
our barque changes sails, turning homeward.

Fashion fades into folds in the glimmering sun
and locks rusted shut swing wide open
while the wind of the mind sways the stars, and
our barque changes sails, turning homeward.

Mary Bradish O'Connor

PRESENT MOMENT, ONLY MOMENT

Greens and cold air and a cracked ceiling seen
from below, floating slowly through doorways
and darkened halls, bam, brown doors swing
open and I come to rest, the first day's

surgery. She smiles and lightly lays
a plastic hand upon my breast, tells me
think of some place beautiful. Sun's rays
through ferny redwood branches, an old tree

grandmother. Closing my eyes to see
her well, I sink away from silver tools
and trays and doctors' hands, my body free
to swim forever in deep emerald pools.

Someone's moaning oh oh oh. Recovery.
Waking pain, wrenching sounds. Oh God, it's me.

SAY YES QUICKLY

Get over it. There's a tear in the fabric
of forever and it's just the way
it is. God didn't tap you on the back
because you were a bad girl and today
you pay for it. You did nothing wrong.
It wasn't all the walks you didn't take
or Irish luck that tossed you headlong
into cancer. Consider this a wake-
up call and live your gift of days with joy.
Walk the edge where air is thin and clear,
where fear can take you further. It's just
another country. Chin up. Step through the door.

Each breath in a miracle.
Each breath out a letting go.

EVENSONG

Now
earthly things
step back
into shadow,
shades
slipping into
darkness.
The eye doesn't see
but the heart knows.
You must look away
to understand.
Let it go.

Now
there is only
the window
and your breath
upon it,
soup steam,
light gleam.
Life stands outside
in silken silence
wrapping
tree arms
around you.
Let it go.

Now
there is only
now.

JOURNEY

Twilight ocean
swells and foams
while you walk
*

along the headland trails
and whales swim south
for the winter.
Everyone is almost
home now
where Christmas lights
shine long into the night
and gifts wait to be brought
to life tomorrow.
It is the eve of Christmas
but the sun doesn't know it.
She does what she
always does, sinks
and glows for a long time
afterward.
Roses. Violets. Gold.
Hold this moment like hot coals
in a cold bed.
All your Christmas Eves lead
to this one,
a wild winter ocean,
the sun just gone,
gifts waiting at home
all for you.

IN COUNTRY

Tet happened on a pink TV
in the Mission District
third floor walkup.
Martin and Bobby died there too.
Charlie Company came after work
with tuna casseroles and tokes.
Then ghosts played golf
on the moon and we thought
nothing could amaze us
ever again.

Cut to:
a Midwest farmhouse,
horses nickering and grazing outside
a lighted bedroom window.
Inside the yellow room a woman watches
Saigon fall. Twisting bodies
drop from overburdened helicopters.
Dust and confusion.
Weeping and despair.
Not long after the last helicopter
takes off from the rooftop,
the woman flies away too.
No children
no belongings
no money.
Lifting off in dumb disorder,
we all fell down
in the spring.

HOW COULD I LEAVE YOU

It's not as if I haven't thought about it
from troubled time to time
the freedom and spaciousness of life
in a white-walled room and the wood
floors and scattered rugs throughout.
I would play music
and dance
and drink purple wine.
All messes would be mine.
No dog hair on the bed.
No cat crying to be fed.
I would sleep until noon.
I would rise before dawn.

From time to time I imagine
that ordered, solitary life
of silence and crisp white sheets

which brings me to what
happens after that.
I think of a rainy night,
your sweet soft body
undressed, smelling of woodsmoke
and raw clay,
turning toward me, opening,
and I bless this jumbled
windblown day
of abundance and surprises
of dogs and cats
and you beside me
afire with passion
and delight

which brings me to what
happens after that.

THAT MOMENT

between the question and the lie
that flies out of the mouth
without meaning to.
That instant
where frozen energy
thaws into the smooth
untruth.
One minute you're walking
into the room
and then before you know it
you've said something
that you wish were true,
something you maybe made
into a story you like,
but when you listen to the words
as they form
and hang in the air,
as the other person takes them in,
*

you know you've twisted
and turned away
from the truth of the thing.
In that moment
you've created a living
intracellular accomplice
that will never leave
you. Like a tumor,
it will feed on the sugar
of your soul.
There is only one remedy:
forgive yourself.
Go back into the room.
Begin again.

PAH TEMPE

Circle come round
to the Virgin River,
canyon hot springs,
Paiute healing waters.
Sulfur smells, rising bubbles
erase a dozen years
in a fluid moment
of dry breeze in cottonwoods
flashing along the stone path.
Today there is a woman
close to death
in the river,
a sack of guts
and languid long bones
and lighted eyes
bobbing inside a plastic inner tube.
Two young women hold her upright.
Small boys splash around her,
shouting "watch me! watch me!"
Later, when the sun is lower,
strong arms will lift her out
*

of the river and carry her
back along the whispering path.
But now
in this blessed moment
we are in the water together
floating, floating
in this sacred place
this blood-red canyon
where hawks fly overhead
and sooner or later
we will all soar.

GIVING THANKS

Two years ago there were hospital smells
and a sweet taste in the back of my throat
and tubes everywhere I looked in that hell
from the haven of the bed, rumpled boat

riding waves of pain. Freed each day from one
more chain that tied me down, I fled
the bed and found that Autumn had begun
without me, scattering doubloon leaves that led

me down the highway home. This Thanksgiving
it all comes back and I remember
my heart's fierce joy just to be living
in that grim and glorious November.

Crimson and gold leaves fluttered before me
as I turned west toward the turbulent sea.

Anna Tui McCarthy

LADY MACBETH DROPS BY COSTCO

No one seems to notice
the blood spattered over my clothes.
The nice lady in line ahead of me
long liquid black hair
shepherds her finds
huge muffins bakery fresh
blossomy like bosoms
out of the way of our less florified plunder.
My hand that had been fingering
silk from China
gray green as my eyes
now picks up the bleached bone underwear
the tapes from Taiwan
the organic salad greens
a mizuna leaf eyeing me suspiciously
thru the plastic.
I make it past the polish sausage
and the pink lemonade and I know
it would be a kindness
if you would beat me
to stop the gnawing of my heart.

THREE O'CLOCK IN THE MORNING OF THE WORLD

INCANTATION FOR MY GREAT GRANDMOTHER SERAFINA SUÁREZ

TRANSLATED FROM SPANISH BY THE AUTHOR

Come a little closer, Serafina, until
I can know your pleasures as a maiden,
because at this distance
I only know of your anguish.

Glioma, astrocytoma, nephritis, porphyria.
Names of the flowers of death.
Names of the stars of death.

Dreaming up happiness in Paracho
the women go from door to door
with guitars in bundles on their backs.
In Zinacantán, they come down
the mountain trail with calla lilies.

Watching the rain fall in Paracho
satellite dishes making castles on the roofs
so that there is a magic elf in each house.
The jungle and the cable and the rain
in Uruapan.

Talk to me Serafina,
because I've just found you.
Because the world is ending again.
Tell me your pleasures
because my throat is closing with pain.

I know that you used to wake up in the night
between the aggravation of surviving
and the terror of dying
at the end of the last century.

You find me here
at the end of this millennium
begging you to pray for our pleasures,
because now we have
war without smoke,
war without respite.

Watching the rain in Paracho,
the water sliding over
the cobblestones in Moorish shapes,
the sadness of exile penetrates me
like the mildew on the walls,
and I remember that
I wake up everyday in exile.

Then I remember that you have
almost a century of banishment.

I see you
floating above the globe
of the earth
in a bluish egg of
light
calm at last,
while it rains
meanwhile
in this county of Mendocino.

You keep afloat
1,000 kilometers precisely
above
the seawall of Havana, Cuba
by means of curiosity
alone.

Sing me a song, Serafina,
remind me of the enchantments
of living
and of dying.

GRILLOS

Tengo grillos de mascotas
En otra vida fui japonés
que perdí su mujer
en los encendios y bombardeos
de la guerra.
Ahora recorro la casa de noche
en mi yukata deshilada
anotando poesías
ejerciendo la adoración
de la luna y del ciruelo en flor,
pastoreando grillos.

I have crickets for pets.
In another life I was a Japanese man
who lost his wife
in the bombings and fires
of the war.
Now I go through the house at night
in my threadbare yukata,
practicing calligraphy,
jotting down poems,
exercising the adoration
of the moon and the plum in flower,
shepherding crickets.

En la próxima guerra vida
fui esposa de un navegador celestial.
Caímos de las nubes y nos estrellamos
bajo la luna de Argelia.
A veces me parece que solo
la congoja
tiene porvenir.

In the next War Life,
I was the wife
of a celestial navigator.
We fell from the clouds
and we saw the stars
beneath the Algerian moon.
At times, it seems to me
only grief has a future.

ESPERANDO LA MUERTE
EN ATTENDANT LA MORTE
WAITING FOR DEATH IN THREE LANGUAGES

Meadow is dying.
I have that thought maybe once a week.
More often I amend it:
Meadow may be dying or
do you suppose that Meadow is dying or
how will I know when Meadow is really dying?

I saw her at the laundromat
under the yellow-green fluorescent lights
of hospitals and jails and schools.
She said, "I need to get some body work,
although Darrell has been working on my left shoulder.
I suppose that they press on things down there,
and sometimes I don't feel like being in my body any more."
I, on the other hand, suppose
that "they" are tumors.
I nod clutching my granola and light bulbs
while the jumbo washers whoosh
like the tides at the Headlands.

So maybe she will die on a Thursday like Vallejo.
Today is Sunday and it rains anyway.
So this is one more friend
I don't get to keep . . .

I wrote:
"The Hand of God—Could it be mine?
This small hand, trailing like the Seine."
But, no, this hand is not small.
It is large, but graceful.
And I'm not God
because God doesn't remember anything
being as He lives in the Eternal Present
and we are not in Paris.
But it is the Lord's Day
and I can't stop crying into my elephant hands
*

which remember themselves
cupping the violet *Cortinarius*
wavy like elephant ears
while my flowery friend
blossomed for me
before my eyes.

I want to become diaphanous.
I want my lawyer mind to go play
with that passionate mouse
for yes, mice are passionate,
if you think about it.
I want to be brave today to enjoy
the toasty pleasures of the fur.
I don't want to know what it is:
to be waiting for death
at an early age.

With this hand-friend
I can almost-reach
the Almost-Dead
to keep them from dragging
so much of my past and my future
with them.

But
maybe, when we are all dead
we'll say to each other, "You know,
we're so lucky to be dead now!"

Carol Kohli

THE BEGINNING OF BEAUTY

Mine is the landscape of the heart
and the
            soul-sweep of our humanness.
                        no need exists
            to plumb the seas
        or tramp the jungles.
the interior panorama presents many climbs and ripe   surprise
of surpassing   interest and   infinite   possibility.
I write the dreamtime   and the mind play   and the vivid
tangle of passions;   the scholar,   the child   the fool!
all are contained   all seek expression   and grow bolder upon being revealed . . .

through expression   comes release—   and understanding   and
acceptance.
as we look within and plant the flag of ownership
on whatever unsettled scape we find
fair or foul   we will have less need   to point an accusing finger
                                                at foulness around us
because we will know it to be contained,   in some measure,   within ourselves,
and, relaxed, can say,   "Yes, I thought that."
                    "Yes, I am capable of that"
                                        —and forgive myself.
I seek the end of suffering and conflict.
I would raise a wand if I could, and wave it in a grand sweep, saying, "BEHOLD
    WHO YOU ARE!"
and for people to gasp and fall down,
enraptured by their own beauty.
guilt
and shame and blame   would have to leave the planet then,   having no place
to hide. Wars would stop
in their tracks. crimes against person and planet would grind
to a halt, and people
would be drawn
to sweet
remedies.

I write to midwife that process.
each arc of the pen is the waving
of my small wand, saying
to you,

"behold, dear one, behold who you are."

SOUL SCRAPED THIN

I am
in the void,
the safe shore of the past behind me. the future
not yet revealed.

words fail me, and context
it is necessary to eat and sleep, that remains clear.
but these are events with no structure, no rhythm,
free from their regular patterns.

my body
floats free aware of sun rising . . . setting
yet untouched thereby.
aware of other markers like Letterman and the 49ers,
but disinterested in any such customary diversions;
they no longer apply
to hold my place in time.

the bowl holding the pear looks as it always has;
all is orderly and ordinary. I go about things in the usual way.
my voice sounds the same and I make
appropriate response.
stillness is the predictable quiet of midday.
no mystery likely to reveal itself,
the air does not quiver with portent.

all is as it was . . . except me.
reality has moved about 1°
to the left   I have not gone with it
or maybe *I* have moved . . .
either way, usual connection is altered.
it doesn't hold me as tightly.

not that any of this is comfortable!
even disconcerting is too weak a word.

perhaps by turns; frightening, anguishing, disorienting, confusing,
                                        maddening as well . . .
only half the usual panoply of emotion parades itself.
yes, I would choose those (words?) with a more positive charge,
but they seem on vacation . . . or now at best, just there
                    around the bend.

I have asked for help.
my attitude? . . . irritable expectancy;   I can do no better.
I await goodness and glory.

over the standard roar of household machinery a great silence reigns.
sounding clearly, above the dishwasher and furnace,
it hangs heavy, like a velvet curtain   waiting to descend,
to shroud one scene,
reveal another.

this waiting feels interminable.
with time scrambled I can't tell
how long it's been,

                    how long it will be,

appearing as if to stay forever—does still another   forever   wait to dawn?
does the forever of the past vanish with some forever anew? . . .
how long is survival assured,
                without the framework of a life to hang it on?

I wonder
is it possible for a soul to be worn to shreds,
disappearing like a ragged shirttail?
and am I not worn fine?
if I were a stone I'd now gleam from this repetitive rub,
I'd polish to a thin blade, fragile as glass . . .
you might see through me,
                turned sideways or facing head on.

fluids now pulse through transparent tubes, funneled in and out to ballooning
    organs.
synapses click. airway sighs. and plastic tendons move crystal bones.
*

yes, a fine filigree, quiet as a ghost . . .
my body performs its alchemy; refining slowly
into essence.

elements hang together . . . tenuously,
their confluence stoking my soul, lending endurance;
                              the glue that keeps body-wisp and soul-scraps
together.

in the eye of the hurricane is utter silence.
it is like that here.
ahead the eye-wall masks a kingdom I've heard.
from here
suspended with nothingness all around,
I see no inference to be made, no future to be known . . .

I await a sign.

Cecile Cutler

CONFESSIONS OF A MAD MASSEUSE

I propose to you:
"Let me touch you.
Let me take away your aches and pains."
You say, okay—
Present your dirty feet
Caked with the earth
beneath your toe nails.
—Reminds me of cinnamon on bread.
I wonder at neglect.
I touch your belly.
—Reminds me of an egg,
—an egg of soulful energy,
full of caring and sharing,
tall and yearning,
reaching for repair
Regeneration.
Stretching, feeling,
Lifting arms which hold
Dreams of love.
Way up beyond the pulse of belief,
Stretching the cords which bind you.
Yea, dance with your
Cinnamon toes;
Unstiffen yourself
And kick the moon.

Susan B. Fraser

HAIKU

Briefly, you entered
Surprising me immensely—
    My unguarded soul.

            Gray predominates.
            Outside, bird songs seem surreal.
               Summer fog is here.

Pugnacious hoar frost
Clings to everything I see—
    Prophet of winter.

            Silver-gray sunlight
            Filters through summer-green leaves.
              A new day arrives.

Two birds wetly mate
Outside my window, raining.
    Why am I so sad?

            Touching, feeling love
            After barren winter's cold—
              Warm and safe at last.

Rain pounds on pavement,
Beats inside my head, washing
    Tears and trash away.

        Pancake-eating bird,
        You visit us this morning.
            Shhhh—don't tell your friends.

Happy little snail
Curled up inside a lily,
    Basking in the sun.

        Little hummingbird,
        You peer in through the window;
            Suddenly you're gone.

Shiny plastic rose,
Sterile and without odor,
    What is your purpose?

        In the sea below
        Hungry seal crying loudly—
            Fish-snatching sea gull.

Happy-sounding chimes
Playing in the wind tonight,
    Will you go to sleep?

Dripping clouds of gray,
Reflections in a puddle,
    Make me want to pause.

                Leaves tumble madly
                Across the busy highway;
                    O! Please be careful!

Looking out I see
Invisible gusts of wind
    Running through the grass.

                Scent of gardenia
                Moving gently on a breeze—
                    Memories, so clear!

Little ant, hello!
Hurrying to catch your friends,
    Stop to eat my crumbs.

                Long hours spent outside,
                Beauty where there was nothing—
                    You in your garden.

Linda Noel

UNTITLED

The pink-scaled salmon
Breathes in lilac-scented
Candlelight
In a farmhouse window
The salmon of porcelain
Flesh
Faces west
A watermelon dusk
And moon draining
Of light
Leans through
Low woven clouds scattering
Above the roadside farmhouse
Where the salmon swims
On the white enameled second-story
Window sill
He swims beside her bed
And she believes
He breathes
Her dreams
Of him

MAYBE THEY COULDN'T MAKE THE SHOE FIT THE FOOT

FOR CLARA AND THOSE WHO WAITED

Bring some shoes to the rancheria. They never did.
No,
All the people waited though.

His gramma remembered
They all washed their feet that day
*

The man was coming all the way over from Sacramento.

They waited and waited.

Finally he came, but he didn't bring no shoes.
He took some paper and measured their feet,
Got their sizes and said he would bring shoes back.

And all the Indian people were glad 'cause they didn't
Have no shoes.

They waited and waited.

He never did return.

Phil's gramma would laugh remembering the story
Of the white man bending at the feet of old Indian women
Who had never before worn white man shoes.

They wondered what he thought.

There was something about how he would measure the foot,
Then write it down and look at them as if to say
What odd and ugly feet.

The old women's laughter is our own as we speak:

> Maybe they didn't know how
> To make shoes to fit Indian feet,
> Or maybe the sight of their feet
> Frightened him away.

SALMON FLESH BENEATH MOON
A FEAST IS NEAR

> That fish
>   in night sky
>   going up river
>   heading home
> This acorn-time
>   names his journey
>   ✻

calls him back
to beginnings
Called back
to a soft circle belly
flaming red fire
Flesh
feeding
an October night
Flight
of fish across
a frozen sky
With skin of stars

I have seen
that same
Star-colored salmon
flickering

In another river
not named sky
But not far from here

Several nights
back
I stopped at that river
and moon
gave streaks
cut by fish
splitting a silver
ribbon of water
Which was
on that particular night
a lean woman body
Swaying
and dancing
the river motion
Beneath moon

KEEPING WARM

On the stretching night of no direction
I wish that voice on the radio actually
Would reach out and touch this hand.
I'm looking for a song to call me home.

This salmon storm, swollen river,
Deadly current gets stuck in my throat.
The trick of drowning the heart. And
Who can help you then? Keep you

Afloat in the torrential motion of darkness?
I am shaking, have too many troubles,
Too many questions, think too much.
My dad used to say and that Indio still says that.

And coyote asks, "What are you looking
For anyway?" And I almost get tricked,
Sometimes I do, because the only thing
I'm looking for is words, perhaps

To wash or weep in or for warmth where
This poet woman shivers. And winter's
Dark hours are always cold. So build a
A fire for yourself. I want to take two words

And rub them together to make sparks.
But they twist and tangle, can never
Burn as one, never become ash. I could
Try striking two stones, but I have no

Stones. What I have is my words. I have
No redwood kindling, no pine pitch, no
Fire pump drill, no flint to strike. So I
Sing.

INDEPENDENCE DAY

real cowboys
& fake indians
walk the hot asphalt
of downtown america
gravel & tar
pave the patriotic
path
of rodeo queen
& faceless brass
march to the beat
bellowing
national pride
the contemporary
cavalry
hail stripes
& medals
but leave no trinkets
as they crush
our clamshell history
with every step
justice parades
main street
in waxed convertibles
& pioneer families
on horseback
tilted stetson
shades
sun glasses
sun burn
& spurs
mark the face
of america
red white & blue
flags
fly high
through staggered
heat waves
and fireworks
false star designs

STREAKED WINDOW

There's this poem about the poet's lips
Graciously pressed on your bearded mouth.

I breathe this dream in falling rain,
A swirling storm, mud slide or sink hole

I would gladly slip into. A near-earthquake
Of the heart. A poem that paces my pulse

Way past the midnight hour. An hour of hours.
And we know none of this. Not yet.

The sleek bare limb banging the streaked window
Is your heart beating my name. And I have

Always been half-crazy, so this added crazy
Is what you do to me. Make me wild, want to cross

The valley floor quick as coyote. But unlike a fur
Full of tricks, this lifting of my lips skyward

is no laugh, no joke, nor lofty line.
The poem being composed.

Virginia Sharkey

NIGHT RAIN

First gear the last seven muddy miles,
meadows unclothed
hills, ravines adrift in dream,
roots tamped closer to the earth's core
not one breathing thing,
Panofsky's barn hidden in cold slumber.

A human one, my hand
on sodden redwood slats
swings the gate back on its cradle.
In the yard, an entire cloud's come down, dripping.

Through the door's glass a single eye
glimmering in metal
welcomes me—the pilot light!
a spark, oh tiny huddling fawn;
a secret, quivering in solitude.

THE HAPPY NIGHTS

These stars,
little salt specks
in the bolted-shut dark.

Two friends,
night strollers,
trace the broken white stripe
down the vacant asphalt road.

Thirty yards over,
left across headlands
the lounging Pacific mulls over its nightmares.

That's three times lucky:
*

to live on the edge,
roam under stars,
and practice being tiny.

RETURN FROM THE SWAMP

Mud cakes all four of my limbs.
My hair feels matted
and the days have silted up.

When you live on the land,
it comes into the house on boots.

There's no need to guess how the sun votes:
it's obvious:

straight down the middle:
days hot, nights cold.

Light finally rids its jacket in February,
the slender month when the mustard weeds rise.

Slopes pare down to lank silhouettes;
evening skims the scraggly hills,
shaves them bare with its lavender thin bone.

EARLY FALL RAINS

Clouds tire of their noble distance,
heave onto sodden rye grasses
& lie beneath us late into dripping mornings.

Sooner than ever this year
the clear blue eyes fled south.

That pact—"In Perpetuum"—the sky handed down
dissolved like Indian treaties.
Some hinge fell,
rusted, perhaps, by all this rain.

Maybe it's heaven,
seeping through cracks in the window caulking
that got itself entangled in the gnarled grape branches
at the creek's secluded canopy

where wild grape leaves, pale yellow,
nipples crimson-tipped,
litter the moist humus.

Offerings:
golden platters
left not for human eyes: these

Blond goddesses
in dishabille; stripped;
bereft in astonishment.

DRIVING WEST TO YORKVILLE, APRIL 3 P.M.

Tons of light off a given day
nap on green slopes belly up to the sky.

Weeds too tall to obey anyone gallop toward the sun.
There must be a place I can go, too, without a horse.

Grasses crowd each other terribly;
shadows under trees widen out clumpy as sheep.

Such a green commotion springs up!
—shrieking, crooked, untrimmed, undeterred

not knowing any better.
It's like this:

Simple is O.K.
The palms of the day warm everything.

WALKING ON THE OCEAN FLOOR

Lids lift from a sleep
where there was no help
to an empty room.

The arms of morning lie flat,
stretched north and south at the Pacific's pale horizon line
where long bones meet
no hands,
no boat in sight.

Since I have lost only one,
and the wild irises are in bloom,
I should be ashamed to think now
of Sigma Rottem's hand
as I wake.

How he lifted,
from underground sewers,
the iron manhole cover,
intending to bring help too late, arriving for no one left alive
in the Warsaw Ghetto.

At sea and air, monotonous gray
lingers way past memory.
Isn't there just one other human being,
like a tangled mass of kelp or a styrofoam cup,
floating toward dry land?

BLACKBERRIES AT THE ALBION RIVER

In the yellow month,
when days fling their doors wide open for our entire life,

and light stands everywhere
like a good father,

pennyroyal stretches out in clumps for long naps
by the river in the meadow where cows doze.

We tip-toe and kneel at tangled canes:
plump, ripe blackberries slip easily to hand,

thorns snag on cotton and the thin skin of wrists;
sweet, the juicy beads of night

stain our fingers, splatter our tongues purple;
squishy succulent stars

brimful of sun
litter the bees' humming place;

a summer's scattering of black dots
splashed down from the soggy evenings

and the flood-wet dark of the rainy nights to come;
a sprinkling of notes inked out

on an orchestra score: the opening bars
to the canon of darkness.

ROAD 19

FOR JUDITH

    About poverty in a small dank house
crouched under waterlogged redwood trees—
white clothes, the pink shower curtain,
even the dog and cats' dishes stain orange,
like the blaze on the sink under the tap's drips;
and three days late after rain a soft splash damps bedding
under skylight leaks as mold finds its way
onto the spines of diaries hidden in the desk drawer.

    About living in a small dank house—
the sun matters vitally;
its habits get intensely scrutinized:
the time it peeks through the brittle bull pine branches
just before its half-hour slant across the plywood floor;
and the sad moment too soon after lunch it slides off
*

scotch broom onto pine-littered fern leaves,
then fades from the yard.

    The one thing left is each other's
thick lives, intertwining and scraggly as huckleberry clumps.
To be a surprise to each other like
chanterelles and hedgehogs popping up after rain;
to be a wide, green place for friendship—
the broad leaves of the trillium,
single calm beauty flowering up in the ravage
of LP's timber devastation.

    About living in a dank, dark house:
you get out of it as often as you can:
You walk with your friend on sandy Road 18 and Road 16,
down Slaughterhouse logging road to the river, passing
Fred, happily soused on his wavering bike,
and Rob the Viet Nam vet, who's moved further into pygmy pines
since all the logging, drying his wet sleeping bag on the wide rhododendrons
using up his veteran's compensation
for gem cutting tools and wild bird seed.

    One thing about not having money:
there isn't much to own.
You see the puddles' gleam
and air that moonlight sits astride.
Some days are really to live for, like when sun
the good landlord who doesn't bother you for rent
peers into the crannies of the late afternoon,
brushes its golden glint into the rough crevices of bark and leaf,
the slippery domes of mushroom and every spindly
lithe, resilient weed that poverty provides.

Marilyn Alexander

UNTITLED

My peers are those who grew up in the '50s,
who entered adolescence as the twentieth
century began its second half,
who had Eisenhower for a president
Russia for an enemy and
Pall Malls, white bucks
Hamm's Beer and Singapore Slings,
hoola hoops, sock hops
James Dean and Ed Sullivan.

My peers are those whose parents
were shaped by the Depression,
parents who saved pennies
knew the value of a dollar
survived the War
stocked the pantry
retired mortgages
planned for retirement—
raised families and the flag.

My peers are those whose children
survived the '70s
bombarded by the promise of
easy sex, the prevalence of
drugs and battle scenes
at the dinner table,
hip hugger bell bottoms
tie-dyes   wire-rims   the
Bi-centennial and
a president in disgrace,
macramé   new math
polyester, peace signs, protests
and cynicism.

Now my peers are those whose
grandchildren pause at the
end of the century,
swathed in oversized clothing
& huge shoes, retro-tasting the
colors, music, styles and fads of
previous decades.
Unmarked by these same wars and wants
they see the future vast with possibilities.
These are the children on whom
we pin our hopes for
the New Millennium.

Leah Leopold

SATELLITES ARE OUT OF STYLE

More than a womb, a nest
to nurture the young or male,
of the species, a woman
has purely personal
longings, redly
livid and lusty.

No longer does she reflect or
project a shining moon, revolving
helpless, in orbit forever, never
to strain, to strive to touch a
shimmering of desire.

50-year-old poem

THE INGREDIENTS OF KLEZMER

The clarinet calls, the fiddles answer, my
daughter sings, vibrates my heart strings
and I see the dancers, dancing over graves,
their feet drumming the earth and the
graves open, six million rising as they
join the dance and I hear the sound,
the weeping and my tears answer and yet—
Is that laughter? Praise God, Lord of Hosts,
I hear their voices through the tears—
triumphant.

"Attachment to God is primarily attained through melody." (Rabbi Nachman of Breslau)

"The Jewish people declared: Nothing remains for us to do but sing and praise God."

EXILED FOR PITY

So young I was, when ballads
of minstrels sounded away
through a forest of silence
and my heart heard,
vibrated and echoed
their songs blended
with mine, filled my heart
to bursting, spilling our
music, leaving my heart in that
forest, dying in black silence,
years lost in black silence.

Then a goddess exiled—for
pity, yearning for home she
blessed me, tenderly
she blessed me,
opened my speechless mouth
to her cup, a gift like fire
shining with melodies
overflowing
down my thirsting throat,
resurrected
my heart strings, an instrument
played by this goddess,
and I sang through that darkness,
the way home discovered.

A BIRTHDAY PARTY (CRETE)

On terrazzo the children dance,
shining glass under their feet,
while rock music blares
and swallows swing
over the roof tops
of Herakilian.

Hibiscus and bougainvillea bloom
crimson and purple on whitened walls,
as the momma serves the birthday sweets,
and neighbors shout news
from balconies, trailing vines
over narrow streets.

Then in a beat, the music softens
to a melody old and Greek,
transforms the dance in a blur
of motion, transports the children,
the momma and me, to another time
here on this street, where burros
and motorcycles sometimes meet.

ON SEAS AND SHEEP, LIONS AND REVELATION

Even the oceans between us
have limits, and from shores
once distant we hear
missiles explode flesh and bone to fragments
washed into the sea,
and inexorable currents
circle the earth staining
our white sands
red.

Those sands are running out
back into the sea
as we putter delicately
debating methods,
while death looms—
a dark giant, eating sheep.

But the sheep shall gather—
gather into lions—gather
the blue heat of fire,
*

make torches
of tongues,
and reveal the wolves
cloaked in gray, silk suits,
wearing smiles
over bloody teeth.

Kate Dougherty

LETTING GO

like an oceantop evaporating into mist:
mist is mist
mind is mind.
Deep sea diver. Pearl.
Misses the fish, the urchin,
the darts blown up
just for him
misses what he misses
focuses on pearl.
Pearl for pearl's part
was only a workaday luminous
subcutaneous accretion of a
lubrication secreted
to ease the itch
of the grit and for this
the pearl is destined
to be target
for a man who will sell it wet
to another who will mark it up 50%
who will sell it to yet another
mark-up to the woman
who will buy it for
a woman who is concerned
it will not go well with her tweeds.
The black rayon evening dress, yes.

Silk, my pearl, silk
is another matter:
cocoons, moths, strands strung
as from a cello humming
when it almost was
an ocean undertow echoed
in the faintest star
the night the moon was born.
＊

Again from the dark.
The gutteral unstoppable
none other
who has within
everything
one can only faintly illumine.

The night the moon is new,
the grit, pearled up, the cello
and one diamond
on the pyramid peak
all lined up
without lines
on this night
the diver dreams he is flying
and sinks deeper into floating
strangely refreshed by the time
the tide let him go.

LAZARUS MOON

Music sometimes wakes things put to sleep.
Put to sleep and laid to rest.
Like a cat is put to sleep
to keep it from pain.
We're not talking sure thing,
given the moon and all, but
there's this space
between the bars of the blues
frees a woman who walks with hands on her hips
and throws back her head
to laugh. She don't care
what you care. She's rhythm's mother
and she dares you—
live. Ups the ante:
never give in.

DUST

Most might not know
dust motes house mites.
A mighty iffy thing this stuff.
If one can know the universe
in a grain of sand
one can know civilization
in a mote of dust.

From whence dust?
Does it matter?
From this you come
to this you go
and in the tidy meantime
we think up treatises
such as this one
to fill the libraries
collecting you know what.

Even the books
will crumble to it.

Sharon Doubiago

SANTAS

My mother has always had a thing about Santa Clauses. Maybe
a fetish. Come the season she begins pointing them out, that's
a good one, that one's not. By good she means the ones
who are true in spirit, a good that manifests physically
in pink square-round cheeks, large sky-blue twinkly eyes, a heart
shape mouth, a nose not too small, not too big and hair
all around the beatific face that waves and sparkles and flows like the sea.
A good one has a real body, no
obvious pillow, not skinny legs. Is large and strong, can hold
at least three children on his mysterious red-velvet lap. Is kind, is
Jesus. *"Now that's a pretty Santa"* is her highest acclaim. I too
have my tastes, I might say prejudices, a kind of lingering
interest maybe not quite normal. There's my first Santa,
the first one I remember anyway. *"That your mother?"*
It is from his knee that I can still see my mother standing
outside the circle of presents, beyond the blinking tree. Twenty five.
Looking at him with her scrutiny. My two year old brother
has gone first, then my three year old sister. I am four
the age she was when her mother died. I can still feel
the electric current running between his eyes and hers
as they stare at each other as if into the deepest mystery of the Universe.
Maybe the North Pole. She has already begun
my daily lessons in the true meaning of Love.
When my father dies, the Vow accomplished to cleave only onto him,
and that first Christmas comes around without him, she finally
tells me the truth about Santa Claus. The closest she ever came
to having an affair. He'd come in where she waitressed,
the Downey Road House, buy Camels from her, play
Love Walked In over and over on the juke box, drink and smoke
the whole pack while watching her serve dinners. She quit,
found a new place in Huntington Park, until late Fall when
Love Walked In again. She was so lonely, that was the period
that if they lived now they wouldn't have made it.
She quit there too. And then there he was on that lit throne
*

in Penny's, the prettiest Santa she ever saw,
her children on his lap. No disguising those eyes, that soul.
What do I want for Christmas? To be as great as she, as perfect
as he. To remember everything. What do I believe? In the
baby born. In Love. In my mother who still believes.

DEER

(deer: OE deor, wild animal: to stir up, blow, breathe; related to animal, soul.)

I've been afraid of hitting a deer
so many this time of year
down from the ridges searching for food, water
Love. I hate
that hunting season is mating season.
So all month I've been telling a love story
on myself and a couple I love
who are coming undone, how years ago the three of us
as new poets and they as new lovers
were returning from a reading on the Russian River
a midnight climbing Highway One I'm climbing now at noon
to her new cabin having just received the news
of your death. *"He swerved to miss it
and the fawn turned back."* Coming around
this steepest, most twisted curve
the buck was just standing there
pushed up against the high bluff, his eyes
flashing red in the lights and, slow motion, I had time
to say aloud, *"oh, honey, don't do it."*
But not enough time to brake or space to swerve
because he did do it, just stepped right out
in front of us, his racks out to the moon and starset
over the Pacific. *"Did you know
deer come down the canyon into your yard
at sunrise?"* you wrote me once of a night or dawn
you spent in the field opposite my mother's house
"just watching it."

The buck was dead and so was my stationwagon.
We pushed them over to the narrow strip
on the ocean side, *that road is narrow;*
to swerve might make more dead. I made the bed
in the back for the lovers with the maroon and gold quilt
the old Mendocino man gave my husband just before he left
patched by his sister from their childhood dresses and pants.
And with clarity, leaving no room for his protesting chivalry
lay down in my bag with the buck bleeding hundreds of feet
straight down to the crashing sea. You
were a man

I could have married
but that you were married.
Love that is *poetry* ignited between us so holy
infidelity was not a possibility. I made
the bed in the back of my car for the couple,
you and your wife and the family you kept making
and have carried you all this way through the dark
to this fawn so in love too she's
turning back into you.

(*For G., for the Baker-Roberdeaus, for William Stafford,October 1993*)

WATCHING MY GROWN SON SURF BIG RIVER THREE DAYS AFTER THE DEATH OF JERRY GARCIA WHO SAID ANYONE HE SEES WHO LOOKS LIKE AN ADULT HE ASSUMES IS OLDER THAN HE

Come into the clearing. He's riding
the wave. His body too small
on the Pacific to be
my giant boy

"You do it for the thrill, you might
die. It's so incredibly
beautiful."

Walk the headland back
around to the beach, study
the many bodies down there. His van
still on top, my lipstick kiss
graffiti-ing the rearview, the Mom's shorthand
I'm around

Back at the clearing five
black body suits
sitting down there on boards facing
the sun descending to the horizon
like some sort of gull formation
or ritual, image of attention
I've stood up for all my life. One
could be him

Then the big one comes
and I know it is.
Riding in, the way only he spins
in air, in water. Then
swims back out

Inside me an adult approaches,
male, erect as a bank teller,
bank pillar, clothes, hair
the color of bank marble.
I've spent my life. trying to extract him, at least
name him, *Father*
Other

of my son's catching
who dives now into the tunneling
dropping like a curtain over him
so sheered in the green flash I know them both again
face down, hands in prayer swimming
horizontally through me

THE LOVER'S FACE IN SANTA CRUZ

Strange how the mind is. There is rain in the middle of the day
with light behind the drops on the windows. All afternoon
a different look on my face. Then that strange
child looks in the bathroom mirror at me talking to her,
starts raving about the look on my face. In the Albion Store
her mom's boyfriend spoke of mirrors leaking. Leaking
dreams. The other side of this world is always leaking
into this one and we are always leaking into it. Embarrassed
I had to lie down. But now the quiet, the dark, all the room
going on without me. Suddenly I'm on a sunsplashed city street
in Santa Cruz riding in a car with you, seeing you crystal clear, framed
in the driver's window, seeing another
miraculous thing about you. You're the same
with all people, you don't leak. You carry your quiet
sensitive self to everyone, to all situations equally.
I'm so impressed I understand what you were saying at Sanctuary
Station, how I change faces, personalities, energy
with whomever I'm with. I always thought this
was holy alchemy, how can one not be altered by the Other?
This morning talking with Loretta in Los Angeles with her mother
who's dying I was clownish, witty, cracking jokes. Few people
know this person. I who know no jokes. She always
elicits this from me, even with her mother so sick. I've always
called this love. Different people plug me into different currents,
for instance you. But now seeing your face in Santa Cruz
I hear those ugly expressions. Two-faced. Changing face. About-face.
Rising up that first hill from the store with the girls and groceries,
the money finally coming, the whole world is gorgeous, the wind
blowing great sunlight over the backs of the sheep, over everything
and I'm remembering how tender some of our moments have been
and I'm in bed with you under the window after a day of separation
in body and soul and heart and mind and the next thing I know
you are crying and then I'm holding our baby and you are talking
to me. Your steady tenderness is a miracle in my life. I see
you really would be my husband for life. What I've always wanted,
what I gave up in order to keep loving men. I have entered
the scene with our baby so totally it is with a start
*

I come out of it as we pass the barns. Then amazed at what I just did.
Is this the way some always are in their minds? When my husband
obsessed on sexual fantasies? When he was totally taken, totally
gone to another place, to other women? Some would say they've
left this body and really are with you on some Santa Cruz street.
That there really is a baby. Is this not love? I can't figure
out my face tonight, the Moon and Sun conjunct
in it. In this moment. In this room. Love, I am searching
for the way to tell you to leave me. Pray
I will always leak.

BRIDE

Nights in the desert I take off my clothes. How long
I have dreamed of doing this. Not having eaten
for over a week—a few boiled eggs, ninety calories apiece,
four ounces of orange juice, forty-five. Something
when I am naked he doesn't like. Humbled as I am
I have always seen my body as beautiful, at least as beautiful
as any *Playboy* photograph. Eighteen, I've waited years
to show him. My mother said daily from the bathtub in the sixth grade
this is the greatest gift a wife can give her husband. My
virginity. He's in the bathroom brushing his teeth.
The trailer reeks of aftershave. 4:30 A.M.
he'll report to work to beat the sun. I'll pick him up
at the end of the workday, 10:30 A.M., our secret weapon
shimmering on the horizon like a mirage, the burnt men
coming from it. I lounge on the bed writing
my maid of honor a post card, China Lake. Being nonchalant,
just being natural, not trying to seduce him. Anything
for him to respond. Is this what I'm guilty of? Pretending
everything's fine. Frying the eggs without butter or oil, I
don't even know that. But I am beautiful. Blue
the veins in the two cubed triangles of marble. In the showers
I saw I was color and shape more like *Playboy* than the others.
But every day since I've been here they have come through
who they were, the visual miracle. Bodies exactly their genius.
Fourteen to eighteen. The marbled fat, the spider veins, surprising
*

bulges and hollows, purple birth marks, the fearful
pimpled faces, pimpled butts, shame in the malnourished postures
under the nozzles, the ones—I knew this only
after you were born—who had already had a baby, or at least
started to. I love and miss them unto sickness. My mother
in the bathtub looked different too, not like the ones
on my father's porno poker cards. She never apologized.
I know you hate me for daring to speak of this, all Greece
hated Helen though she was also God's child. I looked
airbrushed. Every bit as technical as the Sidewinder
shimmering over us in the hundred-and-twenty-six degrees.
I am only trying to find here what was disappearing
when your twenty-two-year-old father found my physical being
beneath him so displeasing. And you exploding out.

THE UNSPEAKABLE COMMUNE OF OUR SOUL

We talk an orgy, the three of us.
The conversation begins as we walk the night town.
She says the conductor worked his orchestra
like a man making love to a woman. *"Yes
do that. Oh, yes, there. Please
do that."* She woke that morning in grief
for the tent going down. Somewhere
in the middle of the two-week conversation
about her past lives as a concubine she renames herself.
Czech names for Spring and Fall. And he and I
the last morning on the bluff so at it
(*"'The walls of my soul are medieval windows,'* Kafka said")
there isn't time to comment or even laugh
when the silver and black short-haired
exposes his huge hindend to our burning faces
as if to say *"here's still another entry to my whole self."*
Nor do we get to, on the broken sea-wracked tree high
over the mouth of Big River, watching the musicians fold their tent,
his unfinished sentence, "feeling in the body,
when, really, it's emotion, isn't it?"
*

other than my "would kinesthetic
be adequate?" There isn't even time to say
love. Only his *"abandoned."* But he's not

my lover. I walk back
alone through the foggy night streets to Psyche
parked outside her house, the world suddenly silent
and finished like the silence at the end of great concerts,
at mutual climax of great sex. We have talked
of everything, we have crossed all the intellectual borders. We
have gone where I expected, then prayed to go with my husbands, what
I've always dreamed of, to meet and be met by my Love
all the way. As I turn onto Calpella
I see myself sleeping ten years ago in this same spot
with my second bridegroom, having driven him
here so he would know the town of my soul. Read now
by faulty flashlight the *Dogs of Pompei,*
the divorce manuscript of still another poet love
for whom his last words were "She needs
your love." *Faded frescos*
of women taking it in the ass
drip with morning fog: . . . I turn to ask
the dogs: "what is my place in all this?" Hear last
the young couple from Prague
arriving at last. Exclaiming "the redwoods so dark!"
Whatever acts were required to prove my love
I performed with submission and ecstasy
and dream the three of us. She, the kinestheologist,
grabs my buttocks, pulls me to her.
She has been studying a method, simple, but so effective

she plans to devote the rest of her life to it.
Lifts them up and opens all my vulva
to him at the kitchen table. It seems years
since a lover has known to do this, my not wanting
to tell what I like, my wanting more
the erotics of learning, his instinct. Only
our alchemy and all its wild dogs and dangling participles.
Despite what the soulless towns decree
I am not talking *menage a trois*
bisexuality or even sex. My body does not betray

my soul, they are not my lovers. I am dreaming
on the bed inside my old van outside her old house, as he drives
the perilous redwoods east to his rental trailer, our need
for each, our human
community. In my sleeping flesh
the sweet orgasmic coming to them
is so exquisite my buttocks are both sides of the heart
fused by the poet's *wine-sweet, dark bread sex*
lifted to the mouths of the Ones
who mouth the Word
to make Love.

        Note: The quoted lines, in italics, are from Dogs of Pompei, *by Robin Rule.*

LOVE ON THE STREETS OF MENDOCINO

In the night I wake from the effort to say over
and over who is it, who
is it? The effort to see him. Hear
him kneeling beside the bed with his hands on top
and beneath my buttocks. I could allow
the sexual wash but quit
that. To wash instead in the terror
and danger. *Who is it?* Why do you come now,
here? Then awake, shaking, a noise
outside. The windows are black, occasional star
lit drop of rain. Wind. I have been in
and out, the outside falling, the inside failing
saying O Love. It felt like you. Saying the names
of my children. Crying. Someone has their hands
on me. Begging who is it? Someone trying to come through
to tell me.

MAIDENHEAD

Coming down the white S curving concrete walk behind
my little brother and sister, Daddy
over there. Through Mama's flowers. The way
images flood around especially sometimes
like when you're making love on your wedding night
he with whom you have made love parked in the hills
for three years but now what's always been forbidden. Sacred. Going
inside you. Letting him
inside you. On the bed back of the trailer in the Mojave.
Three A.M. China Lake, end of June. After the four hour
silent journey from Ramona. The work this is. My father's
grimace, my father's beads of sweat as he escorts me down the aisle.
My mother pinning the bouquet on my bosom. The white satin
dress I designed without a pattern and sewed too small
a failure, big holes left by every false thread let out.
Swimming in the morning in the Navel Ordinance Station plunge,
a buddy whispering go out for Miss Ridgecrest. No I can't.
Hating to disappoint him. No, I'm married now. A new virginity
like my borrowed veil. Going to the movies, what did we see?
I remember standing in the line, the desert breeze so sensuous across
my thighs so bare I'll faint. Embarrass him. Studying
the twenty-six-year-old woman in front of us, dark blonde
in a French twist, seeing how to twist
mine. What on earth
are you two
doing here? Another sailor
demanding. Being
embarrassed, defending
my husband inside. The first time I call him that. Where else
would we be? The first one whispering
lie. You'll win for sure. That it
hurt. How it hurt. A weird
breakage like the way a wall must feel breaking. A
bone. Never again feeling that kind of pain. Dull. Cracking.
Like a dry walnut fallen from the tree when its shell
is cracked for Christmas. Was it scar tissue? What does a hymen
feel like when it's breaking? Seeing
*

his whore in Juarez, "the bitch, so old, don't worry,"
he lost his to. Seeing her wander years later down a dirt road
on the wrong side of the border carrying it. I had
the surgery Daddy paid for. I mean
his insurance. Only a brute, a stranger's face gasping between my thighs,
could have penetrated you,
The first person to ever look there
At least as far as I remember. Since I was in the crib.
In diapers. And that was with sodium pentathol, the truth serum.
As he assured, I didn't feel anything
though I woke up crying out of control. Couldn't stop
all the way back up the mountains. Had to go back down
twice afterwards to be stretched on his table for this.

LADENE

You sleep here? Yes, right
here, that beautiful smile even in the dark, yeah,
pretty soon. Where are you from? Sicily.
Soft, melodic voice. The planet
Sicily. I move slightly in and out
over her to get the whiff of it. Then
let her take me to the nightsky.
"Seventeen now." She's talking
deaths, I think, the count from this sidewalk stoop
of the ice cream shop on Main as we've passed by
in the time she's been here. "Children."
The privileged whiff of unbathed human flesh.
"It won't be long now." Meditation
just like those on their way to the workshops.
How long has it been, last summer
and the summer before that? Leaning out
"I see a new constellation
arrived tonight."

I lean out too. The numinous quality
of the dark. But just the same old ones.
The bright one over Chapman Point must be a planet, Jupiter
*

maybe. (Who was Chapman?) Her smile
is a ray of light splitting the night into two planes, another
world seen in the crack. She speaks
of her children. I speak of mine. Yesterday
walking by I introduced my son. Daniel.
Her smile on him, her eyes the color of the day sky.
Her skin, layers of asphalt the sun burnt off.

All summer I'm astounded by people's kindnesses to her.
"Take it and buy yourself something to eat!" the man
so embarrassed by his generosity, the twenty stuck out
like vermin. Was it the next morning
she was on the bench at Lansing and Main
drinking gourmet coffee (the only kind you can get
in this town) spitting and cursing her husband in the sky
for what he did to her and their children?
Me with my coffee at the wheel pretending not to see this
though I see her bunched-up asleep in this doorway corner
every time I freak for my cramped life in Psyche.

One night she was softly rhythmically moaning
propped up in her faded red sleeping bag
when I came late from the Hotel where the bartender is
my kind patron. Does she never
stretch out? I checked the next morning, the stoop's
not long enough, Amazing the ice cream people
allow her though this is the only shop, really
for children in this town. To allow them to step so near
that whiff. Must be a church project, actual
Christians. She always greets me with a smile
that so disarms me, smile of pure love there's no other
way to say that, but one time maybe twenty feet passed,
the ranting started like an old fashion record stuck
in the groove, and again, like the gruff man
I'm paranoid of my own love for her. Feel a fool
right here on Main, that everyone knows
something about her I don't. And afraid too
I demean her hate. Another time it was
the softest *click click click* after I passed.

There's a sink, the one on the left
in the bathrooms on the high side of Heeser
I put my hair then slowly my whole head into
the icy water every morning now for at least ten years
when I'm here. (Before there were so many of us
I did this at the cafes, Cafe Beaujolais the best.)
Wash my hair in nothing flat, am out of there
and out on the bluff, sometimes with real lines
in my shivering breath, my shining hair.

In that position I stare right into a small slot,
a drain of growing slime from the wash
of State Park visitors and ten years of me, see
what no one else sees, not even the ranger
who comes with his binoculars and chemicals
between nine and nine-thirty. Sometimes
I have to shut my eyes, so close my lashes
could catch though so deep impossible to clean,
but I try not to. Because
of my special position only I
know of this.

MY BROTHER'S KEEPER

There is a moment in my life I want
to make love to my brother. I want
to swim the torrential river between us
and save his life. I want
to put all my body around his drowning body.
I want to pull him into me.

We are in Vermont, our first time alone
as adults. He has come all the way east
across the continent rather than commit
suicide. He's lost his three babies and wife
to his best friend.

Nights he sleeps in his camper
parked on the side lot beneath trees with leaves
like meat turning color. Upstairs
in bed with my love he is out there
like he was when we were kids, on the porches
because it is wrong for a brother
to sleep in the same room as his sisters
and our father when he comes home from the Army
is jealous. To get him here I have raved
about the beautiful college girls of the town.
I didn't understand then
they were mostly Jews and would not be drawn
to a handsome blond cowboy,
Keep on Truckin' taped in iridescence
above San Diego plates.

Mornings our bodies from the same bodies
face each other in a high northern room
over the Winooski, standing
to sip our coffees and watch it
ice-over before our eyes.
He tells me "the big secret,"
the seven years they competed, both making
love to her. "Someday I will win,"
the best friend boasted in the beginning and now
he has, and now my brother's other confusion
about how beautiful she was in his arms.
I am dreaming of reaching across the ice
and pulling my brother to me, to make
the love I have for him actual flesh.
The images float between us so real I know
he must see them too, and so knows
my cowardice, experiences again
love's betrayal. But I am struggling too
to recover from the night with the man I love
who in our high moments begs me to tell him
I desire my brother, to go naked through the snow
to his door. Every morning
I hold my breath that my brother emerges
from the igloo that is his bed.

Our father went around the world to war
and our baby brother took his place
in Mama's bed. We won
but Daddy was never the same.
My brother's legs hurt and sometimes he forgot,
sleepwalked sobbing back to her. Daddy's yells
woke us like nightmares, *"Sissy!" "Mama's boy!"*
Some mornings we woke to our mother on the porch
curled around our brother in the crib.
Now I am like the Nazis
who placed the naked bodies of young Jewesses
on their dying soldiers
in the experiment a woman
might bring them back to life,

In that high room at a window like Vermeer
the white stuff starts falling
around our two bodies of desert at flood stage,
debris of the miraculous flesh
our parents risked everything to make.
Then I am like Isis combing all the world
to put our mother's son back together
so mutilated by our other brother
this is the origin of evil
at the beginning of the world

and I want to be a poet
to say my brother the River and the distance
between us. I want to die
to say what a brother is, to name
the river and be the love poem
to the soldiers on both sides, our
father

to be for all time a line out
into the Nile of his severed gonad
inside the fish that's swallowed it,
rowing, Mama, past our more practical sister
lying down with carrion on the battlefield

my body grown dark as a Jew, the guns
at our heads, the chambers of gas
on every shore, the prisoners
who know nothing now but the fuck,
their mothers cribbed into evidence
against them

and lie down on the cold bronze my brother has become
and suck him back

Patricia Olive Karch

EVOCATION/ABSOLUTION

I evoke my mad elder sisters
Sylvia and Anne
your ravings
were not genteel
your naked hearts
leapt out
red and throbbing
appearing
on sleeves
on hems of skirts
on neat white blouses
they oozed
from shoes and purses
spilled from black suitcases
writhing
hissing
like snakes
The cast down Goddess could not tell you
snakes are holy
and She embraces the Madwoman.

BEARS IN SPRING

FOR RICHARD

When I saw you,
dear bear,
stumble from your den
bleary-eyed and scratching,
still alive after all,
the tulip bulb in my winter
heart
suddenly burst
*

and from my mouth   the flower
glowing red
petals wide
singing like a bird.

COMING BACK

That year I carried pain
like a bastard child until
I left her   my little offering
beside the Holy Well and
walked away.
My tired eyes devoured green
and clouds.
Clouds like islands
without maps or names.
Clouds in stately processions
across a wide, wide sky.

In the dream I wore white
and walked quickly
through thick grey light or smoke
a room of stone
so narrow my hands touched
a wall on either side.
My mother's house
but unfamiliar.
A strange place where I must rememorize
the way out.

SCARLET DREAMS

FOR CORRINA AND KYLA

The day our youngest daughter left home
I went shopping for tulips   10/$1 at Payless.
I bought the last ten "Scarlet Dreams." They
waited underground through the winter of frost
and war for their time of blooming.

I thought tulips were such prissy flowers,
tidy Dutch girls in careful aprons, but
these are not modest.

Scarlet,
as the glossy lips of those girls whose
cigarette smoke and raucous laughter
spilled from the fastest cars on high school
Saturday nights, they open   scarlet
in the morning light   and offer their
velvet centers shamelessly to the noonday sun.

What magic a dollar can buy! (Imagine us,
together, in those black velvet beds,
enfolded and swaying like two bees in love.)

Like Persephone returning from Hades,
like daughters coming home beautiful women,
like falling in love again,
tulip joy is contagious.
Scarlet shadows in the wind and sun
tears in my eyes.

SUMMER FOG

I have always
lived by the ocean,
known these damp days
when fog slips
up the rivers
and creeps
between the trees
and we move
like prisoners
of the heavy sky.

Sometimes, at sunset,
fog slides back
into the sea.
I hurry away
alone   as if
to some forbidden
pleasure   and wait,
scarcely breathing,
pinned
between earth
and naked sky,
for the passing
of the sun.

Again and again,
day after day,
I crave this drama,
this embrace,
this light,
which flares
then fades
into the slow,
deep breath of evening.

SUNSET

This is winter.

Fingers of wind stroke
and stroke and stroke
across dry grass.
Beneath the trumpets
and banners
of a flaming sunset,
a line of brown pelicans
draws its message
across the lavender sky.

No one left alive
can speak this language.
Not even bones remain.
The old ones,
in delicate capes
of the thin and fragile
skins of birds,
turn their faces away.

The wind dies.
Birds disappear from view.
The sun wavers, spreads and sinks.
No sound remains but the hiss
and hollow breath of waves
beneath the cliff.

In this world, I have lost my innocence.

EVENING

FOR GERRYE PAYNE

In the evening, anger must stay outside
the stray cat behind
a politely closed door.

When we eat the conjugal dinner,
you and I always wear flowered dresses,
sip our tea,
converse quietly.
No red fingernails, no snake earrings.
Perhaps we'll darn socks
learn to knit warm sweaters?

Left to my own devices:
bones, shells, feathers,
scraps of cloth, ribbons,
stones, needles,
sharp scissors
no telling what
images I might fashion.
You would invest them with wounds,
pour cups of blood
your words clothe them with power.
We would chant, rant,
beat our breasts, tear our hair.

In the evening the fire is lit   the dishes are done.
It's time for dessert,
but a cat cries outside.
open the door and the lion springs in   a stillness
in the center of her yellow eyes,
her tongue rough to rasp bones clean.

The Danger:
We will learn to love her
want to keep her.

Nancy Horrocks

GHOSTS

Baby ghosts climb on
my lap to hug me.
Unconsoled ghosts
eye me reproachfully,
hopefully.
Laughing little boy
ghosts
dance waves
along the ocean beach,
reach
for my hand.
When you become fully
a man, my son,
you will not
be surrounded
by the ghosts
I see now.
You will have vanquished them
all unknown,
swallowed them
into a whole person—
a man who smiles
tenderly
at his mother.
But now standing
on the verge
anger owns your body,
fills your eyes
spills from your mouth.
"I will take my freedom
from your ghosts
from your possessive
love" you say
moving in
*

to sever
your own cord
with your own
knife.

LIZARDS

I dream of lizards
moving silently
along edge of
ceiling in shadowed
room.
One turquoise blue and black,
the other olive green and copper,
they move down corner
round open door.
I watch.
One stops,
moves toward me
takes my hand
in its mouth and beckons me
toward the open door,
toward the sun filled garden.

Lizard in the fire.
Who is to be rescued?
Son or mother
mother or maiden—who?
It is an ancient story.
If the son chooses
the maiden,
the mother
must die.

I watch them leave
hand in hand in love.
A turn in the driveway
the traditional wave
*

then gone.
A simple moment
this giving over
of son. Though right,
and timely,
it is etched
painfully
on the heart.

But this is not a fairy tale.
The story does not
end here.
It is a story about
a mother's love for her son
a son's love for his mother,
a story not of breaking bonds
but of transformation.
When a woman opens her arms
to send the soul
of her grown child
out into the world,
she frees two souls,
gives two gifts
steps out through
a new door
into
her own garden.

Lorel Kay

TWO STUDENTS

Michelle

Black anger Afro.
Slam white book,
Crash on her damn desk.
Rip cover off
Like skin
From red written flesh.
Crumple and fist-raise,
Defiant.
"I'd like to cram this down your throat!"
Storm black into hell-hall
Of no audience.
Tough act
To follow.

Liz

When she hits me
The world sings out of key.
Purple and blood-gold
In my head pounding
On floors waxed
By my brother's whining.
My stomach burns
To a crisp cinder
In her angry winds.
Are they tearing, howling
At my father,
That sonofabitch?
My golden waves of hair,
Do they remind her
Of his straw-colored
*

Silken beard, brushing
Her breasts briefly?
That no good bastard!
How the hell do I know?
I haven't even seen
A picture.
My brother don't look like me.
I gotta get away somewhere.
The tears stay in my eyewells
Because there's no way down
Bruised cheeks.
Love me, cool guy.
Fuck me, no-name-mister.
My sister and me
We'll bring up our kids
Right . . .
When I'm good and angry
I'll hit you purple and gold
So you won't hurt nobody.
Sing lullaby.

CHILD PROTECTION SERVICES

The ladies with blue-white hair
Nod each to each
And fix the panel with eager gaze.
They mean well.

The court people—suited, men and women,
The social services types—
Less formally attired,
They stare back at the earnest eyes.
The young woman's eyes
Drop to quiet hands.
The panel brings up problems.
Four thousand abused or neglected children;
Four thousand young,
Slammed about and awash
*

In adult waves of negligence.
Parental, societal, Divine neglect.

> I was forgotten for ten years.
> After I heard the gun,
> When he killed her,
> My fear was too towering
> To crouch in the dark closet
> With me.
> My terror stopped my heart
> And I died.
> In the closet, I died.
> Eight years—I died.

> They knew he strapped us
> And hit her.
> They knew he kept guns—just a collector!
> They knew, but they didn't come.
> Where were you, suits and old ladies?
> You mean well.
> But after that,
> I was lost for ten years.
> For ten years after the closet.

The ladies with discrete earrings
Ask intelligent questions.
The panel has answers:
We do ... We must ... We try ...

> My hair is clipped, jet-black, shiny,
> I am small, silent.
> Until the nod is toward me.
> All eyes on me.
> "What was it like for you,
> In the system those years?"
> I lean forward on the table, still silent.
> What to tell the eager, earnest eyes?
> "It was awful!"
> Nobody ever asked me.
> I was dumped in one family
> Then another.
> *

In one placement
They came at 3:00 A.M.
To cart me away
Because another girl had bolted.
Nobody ever asked *me*.

A suit speaks softly:
Eighty percent of our referrals
Involve substance abuse.
Often charges are the venoms
Bred of child custody battles.
We need foster homes—good foster homes.

Ha! Foster homes!
Ten years of strangers—stupid adults.
I'd like to curl up in the closet
Where I died.

The well-intentioned mouths
Are moving, are speaking.
We must raise the awareness
Of the community.
We must *prevent* abuse;
We must try to protect the children.
We must work with families.

I am one in four thousand.
I am dead,
Killed many times,
But I won't die.
I will learn.
I will have a life.
I am one in four thousand.

The well-meaning ladies
Snap their purses closed
And move carefully toward the door.

Lourdes Thuesen

CALIFORNIA SPRING 1997

Hale-Bopp pinwheels across the heavens
with Earth turning back and forth—
fascinated—
to watch her:
our eyes cant to the left or right,
slant back to see her plumed tail
splayed across the light or dark;
computer chips vibrate with telescopic images,
the milliseconds of measurement,
the spooling ciphers of galactic codes.

My cat sleeps unconcernedly:
on the alpaca bed-throw,
hand-made, hand-carried
from the high plains of the Andes
where the twenty-first century struggles
to be born of the sixteenth.

My cat sleeps unconcernedly:
whisker-perfect—
each tuft growing in slow millimeters
in concert with cat heart,
cat purrs,
cat paws,
and cat tail.

My cat sleeps unconcernedly:
while sap rises—
oh, so quietly !—
in moss-draped pines,
gathers in resin globs in the rough bark of redwood and fir;
while red-tail hawks prism the morning sun,
pierce the day's yawn
with overhead cries of hunting.

My cat sleeps unconcernedly:
while this pen receives the impulses of my brain;
my muse graciously unfolds in my spirit,
while my heart delights in comets and hawks,
in eyes and brain,
in blankets and distance,
in computers and trees.

My cat sleeps unconcernedly:
as her heart beats,
birds sing,
heavens turn,
grasses grow,
men toll,
women love,
and I sing the glory
of this lovely morning:
Life.

HOMER, I WONDER . . .

When rosy-fingered dawn
—like this morning sliding over Mendocino hills—
warmed the eastern sky,
beneath the walls of Troy
the men would stir
and rise
and tell companions of tents
it was a good day to die.

But did they feel that,
though,
in that early glowing hour
as they rubbed the sleep from eyes
and ate their cakes of wheat with broth
and glossed the bronze of shield and helmet
with a well-worn cloth
and picked away with heavy fingernail
*

the last dried specks of blood
on sword edge or hilt?

Did they not long to say
—in those oath-bound hearts—
but, rather more,
it would be good to live:

To fold up camp and embark
without delay or booty
on those stalwart Greek ships
and head for home;
to climb the rocky terraces again;
to tend the grapes;
to smell the fragrance of the pines of Arcady
wet with dew
in a home-warm morning;

to gather into warrior-scared arms
the lithe and loving bodies of daughter and son
rosy-cheeked and glowing
who would bury their heads in a father's chest
like chicks
burrowing into the soft under-belly down
of the father eagle?

And as the sky lightened
into purple promise of day,
was the call to arms
—to die that day—
as sweet as the longing for home,
for life?

PRESENCES

On The Closeness Of Almost
Driving Over An Ocean Cliff Under The Full Moon
After A Poetry Reading

Your mercury brightness confuses me,
breathes humanly over my shoulder
like an unseen earthly presence,
turns white tide-lines into soil furrows
and pulls me to the edge of cliffs
to walk on water.

I stop short,
shaking,
to peer timidly from under the tiny roof of dark
to affirm your solid shining in the sky.

Indian spirits glide down the dark ridge of mountain
in grey fog moccasins;
poet voices echo—
ringing, calling, intoning—
in the whorls of my ears.

This night world swirls with powers
welling up from gnarled roots of damp-soft redwoods
and water-hoarding dune grass,
dissolving the boundaries between your ghost light,
my body and the Earth.

My car pushes against the whitish glow of light
hanging over the ribbon of highway
where cows—shining, black and silver along the fence—
watch with fluorescent mauve eyes,
their udders filling with thickening cream in the dark.

Quicksilver flows in my veins,
my powers struggle to focus on the comforting mottle
and hum of gritty asphalt.

You drive me further to the pier,
then,
where my heart slows its beating
in the hard sound of rock and wave
and tangy taste of salt in whitened hair.

The clock moves a slow few moments
beyond the seductive second
when I would have lain tangled in kelp
showered in bloody shatter of glass
rolled by blue white waters
sloshing and pulling
at the foot of the sacrificial cliffs.

WINTER BERRIES

At night I check the strawberries.
The cat—
back curved and compact next to the window—
watches me from inside,
her beige fur luminous with the yellow green and red
of the Christmas lights.

Four clay pots sit one to a step on the threshold.
This New Year's night
the sound of heavy occan and chorusing frogs
fill up the whole of the salty dark air.

Flowers are white stars.
Leaves scored deep green
and berries ripen in this winter weather.

The rain has doused them well
and deer disdain cement beneath their delicate hooves;
so they grow,
unseasonably it would seem,
under a sky glittering in Orion
with all the magical spirits of winter solstice passed.

Ripe they are and red,
rounded, globular,
textured with tiny yellow flecks—
pollen dusted?—
hanging precariously over the lip of pot.

But sweet?
In this untimely season of years passing
and age creeping into bones and muscle?

Yes, Sweet,
juicy with the full season's measure
of life and mystery.

Julia Doughty

THE BEAUTIFUL GOWN

The beautiful gown kept in a trunk hangs now from a dead branch.
The white fabric, torn, soon falls. It will flourish, changed, deep in earth.
A fullness of leaves borne from the ground.

Write, when the spoken words hurt, when the echoes ring
'til you feel you're going deaf; write back in the particles of sand,
the length of the sea bluff, the width of the tree trunk.

A quarter moon and few stars. When the door opens,
it's possibly below freezing, or a warmer night.

The trails I walk all have the mark I leave—
I walk with the longest of veils, so long and old, handed down generations.
I think, I am not this, I am that;
or I *am* this, I am not that.

A little red paper rocking horse is in the corner of the room.
Always smiling. I know I can't ride it anywhere.

I have been waiting. Waiting, waiting. Even when you walk.
Or as she talks. No matter who, how.

In the South I visited real flesh and blood family. In the Northwest
there are archives preserving a portion of the family's past.
At the end of California's coast is a place I used to call home.
I am waiting for my taxi to arrive.

Pull out the vows, like a drain to a warm tub, and what have you got?
Try your strangest compost in the poorest,
most depleted of soils and see what you get.

Love isn't the void, the anonymous silent phone call in the middle of the night.
At the bottom of the river are lost rings—
and it doesn't matter. I'll walk the bridge, drive through potholes of ice.

So much to avoid along the way, and grace alone as companion.

SALLY BELL, THE "LAST" SINKYONE

you came into my home
and killed my grandfather
my mother and father
my brother
and i escaped into the brush
and you cut out
my baby sister's heart
and threw it out
where it landed near me

i held it
that heart
a long time

when

you were already gone

i didn't move
i felt so bad

later
i ran into the beautiful woods
later
i found a few others
we all felt so bad

we didn't dare
build fire
you might come again
for us

we ate anything
we could get
berries   roots

when
we didn't have clothes
after awhile
we slept
under fallen fir
and
in hollowed redwood

we
didn't have
anything
of our own

to cover ourselves

Blake More

HONEY MOON

Marry me moon
and I will wrap myself around you
like a gown of sun
love your shadow
as much as your pearled mirror
never forget you when the sky
—tired of your glory—
calls in the clouds

I long for a lover
who isn't afraid of my howling
sees my waxing and waning
with equal eyes
a mate who lays with me some nights
leaves me alone on others
always offers a sliver to hold onto
the changing tide
my womb

Marry me moon
and I will never be lonely again.

WHY I LEFT DODGE

All Marin County does is talk
you say, rushing along
on your own private Ganges
and finger paint cosmologies
I listen, phone strung
between car and shoulder
both hands flat
against the fever
of my favorite mug

I want to ask
if you saw the moon last night
or if the 9 am sun is painting
your bare thighs gold
as it urges the cherries
into bloom
instead, I let you rant
not wanting to sully
your soapbox like everyone else
become yet another
excuse for tears
and lonely ascensions

restless, I pick up my new pen
run my thumb along the carved wood
hope the check that paid
for it is in the mail
my neighbor feeds his rooster
I watch its red chin disappearing into seed

and you squawk on
something about an important party
insisting we go together
so they can see what's happening to you
I ask why me
you sigh like rolling eyes
remind that I'm a witness
to the *psychic restructuring of your consciousness*
I don't laugh
not because I know you're serious
but because you've told me
how it feels to be you
I muster maybe, trusting
your THC-marinated memory
will overwrite this conversation
lure a more innocent voyeur into your debut

It doesn't matter because already
you've launched into mystery school rap
absolutely no absolutes
*

and your trinity—a future
of three books, packed workshops
a healed flock

I picture your invisible mentors
realize your pendulum act
might make you a Best Seller
take you all the way to *People* magazine
your face familiar to millions
of readers like my mother
who'd be proud to tell her LA friends
she met you over a latte in Sausalito
who'd want to know
why I don't have your ambition
forcing me to repeat
what I once tried to tell you

I would rather
dig in the garden
plant carrots
chew from the earth in front of me
wait patiently for tomorrow.

NOT MEDITATING

All attempts to meditate are the abject denial of it.
—Krisnamurti

Sometimes when I sit on the ground
for no reason, bills paid
deadlines met, stomach
neither full nor empty
my quiet spreads and fills me with sky
from brain to big bang
I am the blueprint
a marriage of flesh and sapphire
discovering the opened eye

Sometimes, I become the laughter
of sunflowers or tickling bees
I grow louder than sirens
the dogs howling
from their backyard prisons
I forgive the intersections
that haunt me, face
after ink-toiled face
sealed behind glass
unaware that even seatbelts
can't save them

Shhh, I say
the snap of breath against spine
the echo of saliva
moistening this heartbeat
calling me back
to right here
to the size of myself
where I don't have to remember
because my funnel opens
and stars pour cream
into these bones
inviting my arms
to wrap around
all that is everything
and squeeze

MAKEOVER WOMAN

There are days when I want to be a Woman
to know others like myself
without the trespasses
of culture, of competition
betraying our birth
where the mention of our name, our sex
is a baptism.

Days like today, in writing class
considering Celina's memories
as I watch her fingers curl in starless hair
noticing how light travels from her eyes
to cast perfect shadows on her cheekbones
how her ample lips kiss and rub each line.

A sudden puffing in my cheeks
my lips thinning, my eyes less alluring
I follow as she finds Calcutta again
relaxing when her young stabs
disappoint the India I remember
subtleties of magic missing
from her obvious streets
nothing of sunset mounds
rising from walkways
in hues of cumin, marsala, nutmeg
or brown bones barefoot atop brown dirt
moving still in air unpaced by time.

But this is her spotlight
not mine
and a sky-like knowing begs me
to step aside and listen
release the contest
ride on her breath
admire her gangly words
the way she stops and barely fills her lungs before speeding on.

Wanting, I shake off my training
my image, and, for a moment
barely a moment
her perfection and imperfection join hands
and I become mama chicken
sleeping under her bed in that village
running out in clucks
as her face lifts to daylight.

I see a goddess alone
then a cauldron of us
*

wise women boiling up from the earth
watering our dreams with tears of blood
young voices, old voices
loud shards pulled above ground
cracked and unidentified
yet witness to a sisterhood
who honors her cities with speech
mothers and daughters life has not forgotten
still living together
without fear, lack or measurement
equality not just among men
but among women.

I want it forever
a vision bold enough
to wrinkle the hillsides
with the ripening of all Women
quiet my panic
as the roses touch her hands
crown graces her head
her with the youth, the men
the magazine covers
me wasting in age and wisdom

Today, she is winning
only to learn how to lose.

I am too.

And again, I want to be a Woman

BOY-MAN IN THE CITY

Another man made by Hollywood walks on my sidewalk
Redwood tall, tennis court doll, his cheeks whittled from iron
then masked with dry wall. Gorgeous is his uniform
as it looks across the street, away from mine
till distance protects him and I catch him
reassuring his profile in a shop window.
*

Like me he sees well-manicured flesh,
purled arms, Levi legs,
long coarse swell on hold behind five easy buttons.

Twenty to forty, he's like all eighteen-year-olds stuck in aging bodies.
A four wheel drive, rough terrain, all purpose guy, he carries
a tread of mud three winters thick around his boy-shaped heart.
He drives fast, skis faster, loves fastest, knowing speed as his ally
since speed takes him from one action to the next
without the possibility of his getting caught in between.

To him in between is boredom, or worse, suburbia. Death
and a townhouse overlooking some dogshit greenbelt,
a two-car garage, two kids, two mortgages and a relationship
with a woman who isn't afraid of his fear or her own.

So he looks, he smiles, he gets another phone number
and he sweeps that one off her feet until she falls.

Sometime later he confesses to his surfing bud that she'd been the one.
He recounts the round of her tits, the vanilla scoop of her ass
the way her tongue curled on him. Her smell, her taste, her noises.
The time they did it in the service kitchen at the Fairmont. Over a beer
he whines about how she married some fuck lawyer and moved to Marin.
If only he'd known, he could have told her. He could have loved her.

He goes home and withdraws from the one he decided
he was falling for a month ago. The balance tipped
since the afternoon she poured coffee into a cup and handed it to him.
She'd left a message on his machine. It may have said "I love you."

Sometime later he confesses to a regular at her cafe that she'd been the one.
He remembers her cinnamon lips, open and full, the teardrops in her kiss
the stuffed zebra she kept on her dashboard. Her smell, her taste, her noises.
The time they did it under the counter, under her boss's nose. Over a latte
he bitches about how he saw her last Sunday at the Paradise with some poet-fuck.
If only he'd known, he could have said me too. He could have loved her.

That night he meets Monica at the corner of 16th and Valencia for a falafel.
Her empty fingers swing by her side and she asks him what's the matter.
He says nothing, he's just tired, that he'll call her over the weekend.
He walks her to her bus stop but doesn't wait.

Sometime later he confesses to a bartender . . .

Karin Bruhner

LISTEN TO ME

Listen to me
Not with your ears only
But with your heart and soul
Listen to me
By opening up your heart
And let me in
Embrace me
With your thoughts and wisdom
Open up your heart to somebody else
By listening to them
Keep on filling up your heart
With other peoples' voices
You can feel their souls in your heart
When your heart is getting full
Empty out all impurities
Of the past and present
When your heart is full again
Your soul will be full
Of peace and harmony
For now and forever
People will listen to you
With the feeling of warmth in their hearts
Because of the love and care
That form each thought
And how tenderly you express them

R.W. Oschin

POLIO

muscles contort
white-coat confusion
deafening epidemic

I awake
behind steel
bars
paralyzed

now, rosined horsehair bow
scrapes wound strings
corduroy cello
slows my gut to a moment

how I yearned for this
stillness
burying my head
under my pillow
alone that year

SHEAR

a snip of philodendron
all I took when
leaving my husband

now barefooted in spring sun
I wash soil from its roots
trim long vines and

wonder about cutting
my hair again
after all these years

I LIVE WHERE

there's no need
to check the back seat
of the car
at night

the fog
creeps in
silence

the line
in the middle of the road
runs out

our journey
is as solo
as the stars'

Patricia Moore

DISPARITY

Entre
　　le rêve et la réalité
　　le bonheur et le remords
　　le désir et le devoir
　　　　　il y a nous.

Toi, qui es partagée entre
　　ce que tu crois est ton devoir
　　et ce que tu découvres est ton désir
Toi, qui es déchirée parce que le bonheur a
　　toujours pour compagnon le remords

　　　　　et

Moi, qui vois en toi mon âme-soeur
　　et qui rêve de vivre à ses côtés
　　mais, qui accepte la réalité de cette
　　　　　impossibilité.

LE VIDE

Tu me manques incessament
Incessament tu me manques.

Je ne pense qu'à toi dans mon ennui.
O que l'on puisse en être délivré,
du désir qui vers moi t'attire.

C'est le démon du souvenir qui cause le malheur;
Que l'ange de l'oubli me rende le bonheur
d'accepter paisiblement que je dois vivre loin de ta présence.

O toi qui me manques incessament
Que fais-tu en ce moment?

Devreaux Baker

PRAYING FOR THE FISH

In my memory the dimension of the room is unclear,
the colors blurred, distorted, what I say is blue
could be black, what I remember as yellow
could be red.

There was a girl sleeping on a bed in one corner
against the wall
there was a man standing, no, bending, over her form.

The night was still, trapped like the holy ghost
in the imagination of a child
straining at the borders of the day
wandering its portion of dark.

This is not a fairy tale
there is no happy ending
the man is a stranger to the girl
while she sleeps, he watches
she does not know her life is about to change.

When she is pulled up like a fish,
gasping in the still night air
it is the weight of his hands
hauling her up and up
she remembers later.

Sometimes when she tells the story
she can feel the weight shift inside her chest
like a huge sack of rocks grinding against
her form.

This shape reminds her of the gunny sacks
her father hauled from the bottom
of the boat,
filled with fish, struggling to swim right off the dock,
the way their mouths
*

gasped for water, the way their eyes
slowly froze beneath her touch.
And she remembers praying
to the God of the Wet Things
to take them back under
the green waves once again.
She watched as her father
emptied the sack on the pier
and the silver bodies flipped up and down
for what seemed like hours
believing they could
swim in air.

Sometimes when she tells the story
she leaves out the part about pissing her fear
on the floor when the man grabbed her by the hair
and pulled her back into the room
and she knew she was trapped.
Later she tells the part about choosing life,
about hearing her mother's voice, tiny as
a piece of chipped bone
circling the edges of her mind.
It didn't matter that her mother was in another country
she heard her voice and like a life line she grabbed hold
and stopped fighting.

The truth is she chose life,
the terrible dark curves
the sheer cliffs
the dead end rooms.

The truth is
she prayed for the fish
each time her father hauled their beautiful bodies
out of the sea

and she believed finally in the end
their souls slipped out
through their wide open eyes
long silver curves that jumped
and leaped in the wind.

FOOTPRINTS AT BIG RIVER BEACH

Once at dusk at Big River Beach
I rolled up my black trousers and walked barefoot
to the river, wondering what Virginia Woolf
must have been thinking
when she walked into the water.

And so I did,
stepped into the wet and turned to stare up
at the bridge with its captive cars
everything inside me was blank
there were no forgiving places
no overstuffed chairs
or comfy couches to curl up on.

There was only this endless sky
that stretched for thousands of miles
within me and turning my back
on all that I walked down the river
toward the sandy curve
that draws itself back into land again
and came out about half a mile or maybe more
from where I had gone in
and doubled back to my car to sit
and stare at my footprints.

Later, a couple followed them all the way
to the edge of the water,
the man was wearing very strong plaids
and his partner was in dark orange
so it was like a cry when she kept lifting
those arms, gesturing up to the wind.

Or maybe it was to the cars passing overhead,
perhaps she was waving for help
for the disappeared person
who belonged to the left behind footprints
washing out to sea.

There was something so forgiving
about those bright arms
that they made room for a memory
the exact size of a shiny copper penny
to flip itself over and over

until it landed heads up
with the face of the girl I passed once
on the Golden Gate.
She was hanging onto the side
of the rail and all the strong cars
kept passing right by
pulled forward faster and faster
by the woman cop with no expression,

don't stop to help
nothing you can do
keep driving on through
don't turn your head to look

But memory is like a present
that you can keep unwrapping for years
and even then never find the exact gift,
hidden tiny dark thing
blood flecked or smiling
at the bottom
just sitting after so long
patiently awaiting your arrival.

The wind blowing her hair straight out
to the Bay,
the man walking towards her,
the way he kept both hands
outstretched in front
as if to say

Look, nothing here.

You can trust me.

Really, you can.

WAITING AT THE BOTTOM OF THE HILL

Some afternoons I like to park at the bottom of the hill
beneath the high school and watch the kids come
flying out.
Some are running down the steps
and some are running right down the hill
falling into the street, stumbling up to
head into town,
or out to the beach or hitch a ride to
Little River.
I like to feel every nerve exploding with life
the neurons firing, the cells screaming for more,
skateboards teetering past
on their way to the sidewalks
that face the sea.
The homeless people are their friends, share cigarettes
or drinks in the cemetery that watches it all unfold
day in and out beneath the pines,
the bodies laid out in perfect rows
and wed to the damp dark.
This is when it all begins, when school ends
and the sun is pouring into my little car
and I see the one boy and girl who always sneak out early
holding hands and in this way I have come to know them,
their breathless excitement to escape.
When they reach his truck
he opens the door almost gently
for her, and I feel myself
more alive in this wind
that blows from some other part
of the world.

Like lost children yearn for absent parents,
the homeless men wait outside the Bakery
in some endless repetition
of one afternoon falling into another.
And like the bodies on the hill
who connect us to the past
we tumble head-first toward our futures,
*

as easily as opening a truck door
or hitching a ride to Little River
or drinking stolen beer with Dave,
in the parking lot behind Mendosa's.

SONG OF THE CLOTHESLINE

Sometimes I think I can restore order to my universe
by hanging laundry on the clothesline in my backyard.
I try to remember that clean lines should fit together
just so, you know, towels with towels
and little things with other little things.
Don't mix up the jeans with the panties
because for some reason that shouldn't be done,
but later all day I can look out and see the clothes
drying in the wind
and sometimes feel the water lifting back out
into the air,
and the air filling itself with this wet
from my just washed clothes.

And for a moment the world is not so strange
and there is this song of cotton
drying in the wind
to get me through
to the other side of night.
Sometimes it is all so seamless, as velvet to the touch
as the moles I used to trap, but now pray will escape,
just as I pray the jays won't eat the dog food
the boys leave out as bait
so they can shoot them
from the living room window.

Laundry, hanging on my clothesline
is my sacred place,
my prayerwheel,
my wish for the silence on the grass
to rise and come inside me
*

to wash out the unnamed things
that haunt and roam
and are so frightened of the shapes
of these clean clothes
that sometimes they disappear into
tiny lights, flickering behind my eyelids,
firing blue and green and yellow,
and when I open my eyes
I have been saved by my clothes
hanging so sturdy
on my backyard line.

MYSELF GREETS YOU

Our first night in New York
we got drunk in Harry's Bar,
you flirted with the Italian bus boy
and fell down the stairs
on the way to the rest room.
But before that we walked for miles
up streets I forget the names of,
so you could photograph the way
the tops of the buildings
cut up the sky.
The truth of that trip is, that I fell in love with you
all over again, a miraculous kind of
rediscovery story,
and if I'm really honest about what happened
I can say it was almost as hard as giving birth,
the way I kept struggling to control you
and the way you kept pushing
to get out.
Until by the time we reached New York
there was nothing left for either one of us to do
but accept that we were bound up one with the other
as something more than mother and daughter.

I kept wanting to say I am just a body
with this crazy ghost wandering through
the endless rooms, and you are like the voice on the other side
of any disaster, who talks the survivors through
so they can hang onto that thread of life
until the ambulance arrives and carries them off,
buckled up to some stiff unyielding hospital room board
where you know as they close the doors
and you stand watching, while the thing roars away sirens blazing,
that thanks to you, they are going to pull through.

THIS MORNING THE MONK WAS IN MY HEAD AGAIN

I never know just when you are going to appear
but this morning there you were, smiling,
through the flames of your own body burning.

Why do you keep coming back to visit me
when I keep planting tomatoes
just for their smell alone,

and this winter even managed to plant
sacred Calla Lilies
that guard the property
from all my most hated ghosts.

But I can never seem to shake you out,
like a strong poppy you have seeded
yourself into me, so that no matter

how many times I fall down in the grass
and pray to dirt to make more worms,

and help the soil grow
with my own rotting vegetables,
you will never leave me alone.

Your face through the flames
is smiling, and I am ashamed to say
I looked and looked
and could not turn away

so great was my desire to know
you.

If the truth in this for me
is that I am a coward
or I have abandoned
too many friends
burning with their own terrible
histories,

then please forgive me.
I am listening to the wind
and I am walking every morning
and sunset at the sea.

WAITING FOR THE UNKNOWN BUSH TO BLOOM

I waited for two years for the unknown bush to bloom,
carried it in a pot from the nursery to the first house
you and I lived alone in.

For some reason I can't remember now
I never planted it in that yard, probably because
I thought we would be moving on
as soon as some sign manifested itself to me.

That winter I missed the comet streaking
because someone's son was killed in an accident
and the loss was hard as granite,
unbreakable to the touch
of words.

I got tired of taking care of some things
and drew back from the world in bits and pieces
saving just enough space for you
and the Passion Vine,

And maybe the Bird Of Paradise,
but the artichokes were too greedy,
they gobbled up every bit of anything I had left.

So that bush waited in the black plastic pot
that was cracked at the bottom.
Days I would pass by and I would not even bother
to look in her direction,
unseen, unknown,
being my motto.

In the back of my mind
I heard her roots protesting and I just kept on going
I damn sure wasn't stopping
for vegetable matter.

Then we moved again and our lives changed,
I spent most of my time out in the garden,
angry at the blackberries
and killing old vines.

As a way to anchor my thoughts
I planted the unknown bush once
and then dug it up twice to move it

and in truth forgot that winter
why I had even bothered.

But the world is so persistent
she manages to have her way
when we least expect it.

And yesterday morning I saw huge white petals
bigger than the shape of one hand
trembling and shaking.

And it was true, she had bloomed
unknown flowers and left behind
hundreds more just waiting,
folded in fat green and pale pink buds.

Can someone please come soon
and tell me what her name is?

I think it is some kind of sign
waiting to be discovered
and repeated,

like a story told about Red Seas
and fire exploding special branches

and waves parting,
so a few chosen people
slip through.

M.L. Harrison Mackie

WHAT ELSE CAN A MOTHER TELL HER SON

The stale smoke
of last night's binge
clouds the color
that darkens my
son's sad song,

putting him
deeper into his cups.
My man-child
hurts like a boy
cut loose from

the harbor
of a father's heart.
My man-child
drifts on a current
of resentment

that threatens to
capsize his small boat.
My man-child
is a sailor on
dry land, doing

construction work
in a sea of sorrow
that will take him
where he needs to go,
if he lets it.

What else
can a mother tell
her son,
but to keep his
hand on the shovel

while his heart
does the real work,
staying afloat
in a sea of sorrow
beyond sight of shore?

NOW

FOR JAH

I watch you pack
family pictures, dolls,
make up, sweaters, skirts,
shirts, pants and sandals
as if the space they
empty will hold its shape
in your absence
as if each day you
are away will hold its breath
until you return
as if what transpires between us
when we are together
in the same place at the same time
is not already irretrievably lost
like this offer of my love now, now, now . . .

SAYING GOODBYE

FOR JML

Saying our final goodbye,
we embraced a future
of perpetual blessings—
ripe as Gravenstein apples,
full as mountain streams after winter,
green as meadows in spring, and
clear as the early morning sky
✻

after torrential rains.
From now on, nothing
will impede our travel
because there is clear
sailing in all places and
at all times if we choose
to see things this way.

CRADLE

Comptche's lush landscape cradles the soul
my fetus abandoned in utero.
The midwife who sees her says she follows me
like the moon or a kite waiting to be retrieved.

I ask these days of karmic dilation to open
my eyes to the royal flush the queen of hearts
will deliver my house of cards through hands
ordained to bring new life.

I REEL IN THE THREAD

My body needs headlights
to make its connection
with destiny's direction.
The pores of my skin
must open like eyes
for the heart's vision.

Will I unfold, petal by petal,
to bloom and wither
inside the garden that
grows me even now,
unconsciously,
from seed to soul?

Will fragrance and music
bring the delight
of life's circle dance
through joy and sadness
into wholeness'
delicious repetitions?

I spin. I twirl. I search.
I stop. I wait. I open.
I reel in the thread that
has kept the window
open for You to electrify
my nerve endings.

QUESTIONS

Are You the voiceless prompter scripting my life?

Are You my equator, meridians and poles?

Are You the shape of my fingerprint?

Are You the image-maker delivering building blocks to my imagination?

Are You the shadows following me?
        the dreams awakening me?
        the tears and laughter animating me?

Are You the mirror in which the me of me sometimes appears?

Are You the caldron in which body, spirit and mind
        make an elixir God-sizing me
        to fit the universe of the heart?

Are You the answer asking my questions?

Am I answering Yours?

Dana Ecelberger

FERAL CAT

He sits
at the edge
of the afternoon
wood,
body black as unspoken truth.
Round eyes,
yellow with caution,
pierce the dark drape
of his coat like holes
in a moonless sky.
He waits, patient
as Forever,
for me to feed him.
He has not forgotten
I wanted him dead,
will not forgive
the steel cage
I tricked him into.
Though I have courted
his forgiveness
for a year now,
though he takes my offerings
in secrecy,
I am denied the intimacy
of witnessing even the smallest
weakness.

I hunker down in dry dirt
to watch him,
as if he could explain wildness to me:
the untouchable
privacy and grace,
the absolute boundary
of silence.

A mirror image,
he settles low in the grass,
closes his eyes slow
as the waning moon and
is invisible.

Oh, to be that elusive,
to close my eyes
to the world,
to fade into rustling
grasses and soft tree shadows,
untraceable and safe.

AFTER THE FACT

When I think of dying
I think of how graceful
a bird is in the air:
a hawk on the headlands,
who hovers effortlessly
and with such seemingly
absolute faith.

"If only . . . "
Do not speak these words
to me at the end of the day.
Set them adrift on the stream
in half of a walnut shell
like two play mice on a pretend picnic.

When I begin to suffer,
the colors of the day are lost to my heart.
The world becomes silent
and my eyes turn to the inside
where everything is crooked.

I understand the meaning of forgiveness now.
It is not so much an action taken
as it is a stillness inside.

If I could be still in this moment
with the cool breath of heaven across my forehead
and the moist holding of the earth
beneath my legs,
then perhaps I could be concise
when speaking my truths.

I have an inch in the door,
my foot wedged with firm
resolve.
It only takes a step or two
to reach the water.

When I ask for what I want,
it all comes out like afterbirth:
messy and rich and a bit
after the fact, yet holding
all the riches
in its pearly sac.

A MOUTH FULL

I want to kiss you
with my mouth full
of things better
left unsaid.
To let the multi-lingual
tendrils that lie
just under the lip's surface
tell the tale
they bring straight
from my heart.

Lip to lip
I would fill
the pages of your body
with stories:
how my body aches
*

in the dark moments
before sleep and sunrise.
How mist on my face
fills me
with uncontainable
tenderness.
How my tongue dreams
of tasting
the salt along the curve
of your throat.
My chin would shout
a desire to force forward
through deep waters,
my cheekbones confess
the fear of drowning.
The furrow between my eyes
encloses the emptiness
your absence leaves in me.
Veins in my neck whisper
thanksgivings
for renewed awareness
of beauty:
in myself,
in all that surrounds me.

I would kiss you
as a bird feeds her young:
with dreams, pain, fear, joy
placed ever so gently
in your mouth
to swallow whole.
And, I will swallow
yours.

Johanna M. Bedford

PARTY

I thought the evening was lost to us.
Every glance was received with anger,
your hair fell wrongly over your ears
and clothes arrogantly trespassed,
leaving me out. But with one gesture
you stretch your back, stroke your hair
distracted and I know now that nothing
will be denied and watch intoxicated
how underneath your clothes and skin
your shoulder blades slowly begin
to form into a resting place for the
friendship of my hand.
Still folded,
dazzling and perfect, fully trusting,
they move into their widest stand.

AMPUTATION

A material break as with all life forms
ripens slowly and then suddenly happens (abruptly).
A perfect goodbye is unknown.
You turn around the whole ship, not
just the bow.

There isn't anything you can do or know differently
and once you are offshore,
the right place is up front
where you eat alone.

You are leaving a world that stays the same.
The umbilical cord, tied to the known and the loved,
dissolves in its own blood fermentations.
All this stays and you have to go.

When what you have loved about your land
(and you know how to carry those deep treasures—
scarred, without spilling)
distances itself and collapses,
you find the backdrop has been taken away
and the time to go has come.

No hero's sword picked up
or beggar's cup courageously accepted
but like a sick animal you hide
and feel a destiny spring up
of which you had no idea.

In the glances of friends and loved ones
estrangement is already mirrored.
You get your coat and say you really
have to go now without finding a useful word.

The blunt recognition of known
landmarks, as if the journey is just an outing
and the lost hope with every bend in the road,
both make you want to turn around completely.

You are alone while traveling through
more or less known cities and to
satisfy the smoothness of the trip
you stare as in the movies stupidly ahead of you.

For a short while a dull but unforgettable light
strikes over countries, people and greenery
but then the clouds sailing in from the side
close this view.

BEHIND THE WALL

In the night I am being spied on.
I don't know who is waiting for me.
But when in my garden the gravel bleaches
(night pounds black into rubble)
and I find the morning paper rolled
up in my hand again, I still
don't know what I keep missing.
Is it my grip on the material and the mind
and my fear of it, which will disappear
when I am dust at the end of my life?
Or will I then recognize God as a from-the-
outside-incoming thunderbolt?
His judgment always ends in the death penalty.
That in itself is not important.
That does not make me afraid. I mean,
standing by chance in the path of a bullet
one could get killed.
Will that adventure behind the wall
become as vague as this moment?
All things being equal,
life without me,
me without life.

INTRODUCTION TO EMPTINESS

Today I am tired
and this should be prose
but I am handcuffed
to the train of poetry,
jumping rhythmically, avoiding
railroad ties against my shins
and every time when it is quiet
I ask and look
where this journey is taking me.

Rest is not possible carrying this load.
The night, whirling in its beauty,
squirms under my feet.
Her mouth pouts and
spies with small teeth on my body.

How do I see this? When it is dark tonight
lie down and wait, unknot patience
slow, slowly, throughout the glittering
as a brisk wind rattles the mind.
It is getting dark and dim.
Read a frail picture,
hot purple velvet
in which the figures the most turned inward
become strong, last a while,
break up and mean nothing.
Then when the night fills up
the cavities of your open face
who knows, maybe that last light
did not belong to the last lost woman,
the halls of judgment,
desertion on a dark street.
You drop through the cracks.

And when you don't die in your dreams
what happens with this poem
that lives shyly in your head and grieves?

Inside your skull something big and weak moves,
stares blindly, pale.
A sourceless body hears
me and I am not talking.
It breaks through bony temples.
My brain looks naked.

You now have each other
by the hair,
by the brain,
a stew of thoughts.
They kiss each other and mix
like a wild flaming clay.

Is this a game? Of love? Of sadness?
I write you, write I don't know,
far from your sweet, beautiful ugly body.
I don't cry tears. They don't well up
and they don't find a way out.
You die young. Are old. Have to drown
and I can't help you swell break sink.

And even if you die in a simple way
think how frequently and deeply it still comes from
the outside. Strange that your body listens
better every time to that arriving greyness.
It lets you repeat the scene
that blindly directs you to untie knots.
Clothes fall off. The heartbeat whispers.
Go lie down. Close your eyes. Wait again.
How many years chained to this dormant bed
will it be this time?

NO MAN'S LAND

No man's land. A house with black windows
is submerged in wild bushes.
Children, smelling their flowers,
step over its threshold and the squeaking
of the windows pursues them outside.

Did you see their faces in the windows
pressed together in a long pale
garland? Their thoughts are unknown
to us just as their family names.

How do you know which turns our lives
take: are words sent to us from no
man's land and do a few escape our mouths?

Their black-topped road melts into shadowy
images. Grass grows in cracks. Roofless
dead walls are overgrown together.
*

Our neighbors are riddles and
when we prune the lilac trees
we confuse this urge with wild blooming.

It is safe to wander in fairy tales
and stories. It is easier to dissolve that
road taken than to turn around. Dozing
always ends too soon and in my dreams
I can't be caught.
I am being devoured by a space and time
so brutally clean and wide.
I am getting the worst of it.
Quartered and singing, I scatter
into many echoes,
into a row of arched ceilings.
Every whisper is too much and
too weak to please me.

This way the loving loses itself
together with the hating. Here is no
benefit of a good friend to talk with.
The sea is empty. The ships are burned.
With that silence I feel connected
since I left and left my life behind
that stayed and dozed in that waterland.

Wendy Norris

BAD APRIL

Holding the razor to my wrist every night.
    Citron daffodils and purple crocuses open
        the flowerbeds, I want to open
           an artery—
          free the red, wet animal clawing
              a way out.

Every birth—
      the early sunrise
the apple blossom, the split pupa
      the green shoot—
fattens while the animal starves
         and starves.

Caught in a jawed trap
the smell of freedom, frenzying, says:
      undo the heart, splinter this cage of bone—
         an animal chews through its own leg
          to escape.

Like the slick, crimson tulips
      making their getaway from thick mulch
         this animal will leave red tracks
           on every street while the town reels
             sick with spring.

BLACK RASPBERRIES

Wild vines tangled by the side
of red dirt road like piles of
baling wire; dust-covered, black
noses of berries pointing into the wind
or towards the earth.
Taste like dirt, then
sweet, then sharp.
Those raspberry pies
cobblers, fruit salads
sprinkled with black gumdrops.
Dark chunky conserves, purple mash
flecked with grass seeds in our
Yogurt-tub berry buckets.
We flashed blue tongues
ink-stained fingers and lips
didn't notice the tiny stingers
of thorns, dry little claws
rasping fine red lines along forearms
cheeks, the backs of our hands.
We braved pain for the biggest ones
untouched, dangling voluptuously
behind a screen of toothed leaves
and brambles: too high for raccoons
too deep for birds.
We gorged ourselves like cubs
shit seeds all summer.
With the bluejays, finches
grey squirrels, 'coons—and even
my squat black dog who liked to lip
low-hanging ones off their stems, ripe or not—
we gathered raspberries, forsaking
our neat vegetable gardens, tangled
in their wild black spell.

BLAZE

"What happened to that tree?"

> "What? This tree?" He
> points to a Jeffrey pine
> golden-skinned, sticky
> in July heat.

"No, that one."
Dark Douglas fir
along the brown path
wears a gash, a scraped place.
Rugged bark buckles
at the edges, like a scab.

> "That's a blaze,"
> he announces, how
> a trail cuts through
> the wild black pelt
> of the canyon.

I see how the wound looks
like a mouth, open, protesting.
The lipped groove in the thick
skin of this tree is speaking.

> It says someone left their mark.
> It says no one asked permission.
> It says there was nowhere to run.

> The way my mother after the beating
> by her father said, "Yes, sir,"
> a green-limbed girl, how flexible
> repeating his instructions,
> obedient and useful.

This tree speaks
year after year
the language of scars—
what we can hear,
what we understand.

SNAILS

Her driveway after rain,
a minefield:
brittle shells and pulpy bodies
purposeful in the dark.
Wincing every step,
the crunch and splinter
heels grinding soft, sticky
glad we could not see.
Damage without a face is
easier to forget.

I remember hers, and
that time we fought, not
a battle, more like
fighting to breathe.
Her hard chiseled words
fell on my head, crushing
like a ton of bricks
where before had been
petals.

We made amends in the bathtub.
Hot, pine-scented water,
and candlelight, and
our eyes closed.

It wasn't cruelty, but
curiosity a blunt instrument
in her fingers, probing
my glistening chambered interiors,
wanting to see me laid bare
and beautiful as a moth wet
from the chrysalis.
"Read from your journal," she'd say,
stretched on the futon
while I revealed myself
page by page as if the words were
written on my body, undressing
beneath the bedside lamp.

In the morning,
on the driveway we could read
gelatinous calligraphy,
lacing silver script written by
long soft torsos, tracing their
journeys in the dark.
Between tender bellies
and toothed asphalt, those lines
telling how paths crossed,
how they left
their mark.

"Let us be kind,"
she whispered,
her lips against my neck,
bodies melting where we touched.
"Let us *try* to be kind."
On tiptoe
on the rainsoaked pavement,
reaching for the other's hand
in the dark,
we recognized fragility;
each night we tried
to avoid the snails.

WATER

    Iron Creek.
How it tasted of iron and turned our toenails rusty.
How it ran cold and clear all year long.
How it leaped.
    Rattlesnake Creek.
How it fed forests. Clothed the hills in green.
Made long green furrows in the summer
cutting through gold.
    Corbet Creek.
How it kept our tempers in check
during the blistering season of heat
*

crackling like a white ironed sheet.
    Snake Lake.
How we dove into it, plunged into it
soaked our feet and floated in it.
    Tipi Doug's pond.
How it watered our vegetables and flowers
from hoses, drip systems, five-gallon buckets.
How it trickled from springs or surged
over rocks or slept in quiet pools.
    Shell Rock Creek.
How it was summoned thousands of feet
up steep canyon, stored in tanks and
ponds and Doughboy swimming pools.
    Tin Cabin Creek.
How we turned a faucet and it came.
How sometimes it didn't come.
It was winter and the pipes froze.
    White Rock Creek.
It was the dregs of summer, five months
without rain and the creek going dry.
The line blocked, broken by rock slide
chewed by some animal, dragged away.
    Black Oak Creek.
We learned to trace these arteries.
    Burns Creek.
We searched for the true source.
    Eel River.
We knew where our water came from.

Diane Johnson

STUFF

When I die, it will take sixteen men
To put me down in my grave;
And that's because I refuse to go
Without all the great stuff I save.
One man will carry the blue rubberbands
From all of the broccoli I buy.
Another will cart off self-help books
I always was meaning to try.
One will take from the back of my closet
All the clothes I've long since outgrown,
While somebody else takes instruction books
From appliances I no longer own.

To make room for me and all of my stuff,
My grave shall be wide and long.
The casket-carriers may be weak,
But the stuff-movers must be strong.

One man will take all the old keys
To fit locks I one day may find,
Along with watches, left in a drawer,
That are tarnished and no longer wind.
One man will bear all the old pictures
Of people whose names I forget.
Another will take the recipes I've saved:
All those I haven't tried yet.
Someone will take the weird little tools,
I could use if I knew what they're for.
Another will take all the loose change
I've thrown in a pocket or drawer.

There's a lot more stuff I haven't yet named
That the sixteen men need to haul,
But if they don't take all my stuff to my grave
—then I'll refuse to die after all.

Bobby Markels

MENDOCINO MALADY II

It is quiet here
And fir trees fill my eyes
The windows, the skylights
Are brushed with sun
    and sky and leaves
And I am filled with evergreens.

    The world is magnificent—truly

    I am bursting with sunlight.
       Nothing is wrong.
I could stay in this spot forever
    at my table
    in my house
Under the bursting dome of green and sun
In my very own place
    I know
    and love
For some reason
    I am leaving tomorrow—on vacation

I don't understand anything.

I don't understand what I've been doing for
    20 years now.
It's magnificent—truly.

I walk around this town
I see this town
I know this town

    This town . . .

This town is buried in the center of my soul
Like dreams seen and long forgotten, but saved,
remembered
*

Beneath the eyes my other eyes blind
With reality that's merely real
This town is buried there
Behind a vision so severe
That even God's not sure
Who dreamed it.

This town has arrived.
Main Street is too adorable for words
We have imported coffee and a Jewish psychiatrist.
And everyone is walking around
Like they're the producer and director
And the stage is very busy
The megaphones are blaring
The producers are screaming
Telling everyone where to stand
And what to do
And I'm sitting on the edge of the stage
While everybody's running back and forth.
And no one tells me where to stand or what to do
    What's my part?

I don't want to run in there
in all that mess
And start darting around
And being part of it.
Everybody's very busy and
    Preoccupied
Like they know just what they're doing
And where they're going
With set stuff in their hands
    Bowls of fruit and vacuum cleaners
    Saws and nails
    Buddhas and bagels
    Text books and radios

    What's my offering?

I think I'll just sit here on the edge of the stage
And take note awhile.

I walk down Main Street
The sun is on the water
The waves are white
And it's very quiet
Like it used to be
There's no one on the street
I walk through the fence
That didn't used to be here
To the bench
    Over the waves
    And under the sky
    On a corner of the earth
The bench that was always here
And always will be
Till someone takes it away
And I wonder what it was that brought
    me here
And how long I'll stay.

All my life I wanted to be there
Now I finally got here
Man, you think you got troubles.

I love this place
This land, this country is mine
Everything around me is dear
The certain way the streets look at dusk
These particular people
I even love the ones I hate

(It's all beginning to get clear
    —I think I'm getting it together!)

I was born for this place and this time
And the way the land drops into the sea here
I love the cold grey-blue ocean of Mendocino winter
The cool white sky, the fog
The huge rocks jutting out against the ocean
The silence of Mendocino.

I am through!
I have absolutely had enough.
The hotel is Mendocino's Sistine Chapel
I'm leaving here I can't stand it
Canada, Oregon, Mexico—
Even Chicago is beginning to look good.

They can take their sewer and stick it

Where does an alien go to alienate himself
    in Mendocino?

Listen, when I came here
I knew just who I was
And where I was going
It took me nine years to get this confused
I even knew more five years ago
Than I do today
And twenty years ago
I knew everything
    It was magnificent—truly

I had a lot more friends
I was prettier too
And thinner
It's all right Ma
I'm getting it together.

Most of the time
I have a terrible pain in my heart
And a lump in my throat
Nothing works right
I cry when I sneeze
And if I cough I wet my pants
Everything is terrible
And I am really lonely
Nevertheless,
I'm getting it all together

I'm wobbly, I'm woozy
I'm awkward, I'm slow

I'm a late bloomer!

But I'm part of the show—
I don't know my part
I don't have my lines

But I'm coming along
I'm doing just fine
It's O.K. Ma.
    I'm shlepping along
    Just singing my song
And I'm getting it—
I'm getting it
I'm getting it all together.

I'm a fierce flower blooming on the slopes of Mendocino.

OLD LADY'S LAMENT

I sit here at my table
On my chair
Under Koo Koo's lamp
(He was a sweet man but ding-a-ling)
And I'm gonna figure it out.

When I came here there were blue flowers
And my kids stood on the fence howling at the moon
All night like cats in the dark.
You're all crazy, the old woman next door said,
All you hippies staying up all night and
Going out on your trips.
It was quiet here before you came.
Her name was Billie and we called her
    the Old Lady on the Block.

After Billie moved away
A paper came in the mail one day
Saying they just wanted right of way
To a little spot in back of Billie's house
    —and water rights—

I said, looks like you're planning to build 4,5 houses.
Hell no, why that won't be 50,60 years yet
I hope not, cause that's where I put my garden.
Little lady, as long as there's breath in my body
That's your garden, and I'll see to that.
His eyes were blue, like the blue in Koo Koo's lamp
And the blue flowers in my garden.

When a man talks to you about money or love
You better remember he's lyin.

Now tall weeds grow around the big tree
    in my front yard
Its knuckled arms stick out all going the wrong way
Now on this block there's cars
    friends cars
    kids cars
    trucks
    relations
Grinding wheels and dust flying
And in the back new neighbors plunging through
    huge limbs
    branches
    brush
Stuck a white prissy garden gate
Where my garden was
The exact spot.

Well, it never was your garden, my friend said,
    Don't you understand?
That's not the point. I thought it was my garden.
    And It thought it was my garden too.

Last night and the night before there was real loud
    Rock music coming live from Billie's old house.
If they don't stop today I'm going over there and say
    I can't stand it and I'll get some other neighbors
    to go with me.

    You get to play 'em all.

I thought I'd sell the house but the man said
Where is your garbage disposal and your laundry room
I said I catch the moon every night from my loft
And leaves whirl all day across my window.
You don't have a linen closet either, he said,
        where's your hot tub & your carport?

I sit here and smoke a joint
And drink Olympia light, My God
He said, don't offer me that dietetic piss
(He was another one, but koo koo)

(They were all koo koo.)

My son's wife don't like to cook
She goes to exercise class
My daughter joined the Unitarian Church

I think the thing to do is
Lie in deep grass a lot
Look at the sky, sit by the ocean
Walk in the woods
Keep your eye on the blue
Use the back streets
And stay close to home
You just have got to realize
People get older
And things change.

L'envoi

I finally got it all together
And now my skin is falling apart
Should I sit here and get wise
And wrinkled like an old Indian
        Or have a face tuck
And go out for another rumba?

Eleanor Kellner

DEATH-WATCH ELEGY

TO MY BROTHER

Take his body gently
Tenderly lay him in the earth

Let not the blanching fire of cremation touch him

The cancer's silent white flame
Has eaten his flesh away

Just before they burned them
In Auschwitz
Treblinka
Maidanek
In bunks, tier on tier
Their cadaverous bodies lay
Weakness . . . skin and bones

Don't burn this body again!

Let the earth take back its own
Let the dust return to dust
Cradle him lovingly
Like Abraham, Isaac and Jacob

Be soft, be gentle
Take him tenderly
And lay him in the earth

He was a loving man

GRANDMA REBECCA

Arms too filled with packages to open the door
Candied orange peel for the little sister
Crusty bread and storytelling for all the family

Hair pulled tightly into a knot on top of her head
Huffing and puffing with climbing the stairs
And slow of step

Early in the morning
She brought me water in a basin
"There are little devils in your fingernails
Be sure to wash underneath and around them
And then you say your prayers"

Ready to laugh, but not much scolding
She loved you for you
Sitting at the window reading her books
She was always there

In the dim light of a Harlem kitchen over 75 years ago
She bent over the cookie sheet
Together with the little girl
As they pressed their fingers into the raw sugar cookie dough

SHABBAT: THE PAUSE

On this speed-crazed highway we call life
It's hard to stop
To savor the moment
When you see a hillside ripe with color
Rosy-white wild sweet-pea blossoms
Or the bluish-lavender outline
Of the distant horizon
Through the mist

Last week and every week
So crammed full of agenda and errands
*

As if it were a town hall meeting
Led by a panel of "experts"

Where was that vast immeasurable space of time
That exists without beginning or end
Surrounding me with its meditative loveliness?

When we wrap ourselves
In the holiness of the garment called "Shabbat"
We loosen our connection
To the stranglehold of our daily chores
Those housekeeping routines and tasks
That engulf us
And take our breath away

Theresa Whitehill

THIRST

Rachel drives down to the river.
It's not very late.
She can find her way home.
She's a mystery in the heart
of the center of god.
She drives with a thirst, enters curves
with the ballast of her thigh, ripping loose
walnut leaves from the open window. The radio sings
tall icy glasses beaded with sweat. Snaps her
fingers; forgot her sunglasses. Snaps again because it sounded
so good the first time, then left hand signals, for the river,
the river she must go to today.
Drink from or be forever innocuous. Deep thirst
isn't satisfied with obvious beverages, with
spicy candor, or the busy thrusting of business.
She would be satisfied with a few
colorful lies, a slant-eyed version
of Genesis. Perhaps he never intended
that Eve be so reticent. Rachel would have taken
the whole damned orchard of apples, rolled in them. By the time the water
comes in view, she is digesting the trees, and the spaces between
branches, watching the flowers switch colors,
then evade color altogether, wipe the sky of its blue.
Children and dogs on the mud bank
through which the water flows unique.
Slowing down the green sedan, sliding forward
on the hot plastic seat, she watches the rope swing
glide forward so cleanly, she expects the sky to rip
behind it. Reaching for her sunglasses,
she remembers that she left them home,
and recognizes the first phases of happiness.
The drenching has happened. Something in her throat
has slid to the belly pure. Putting her sandled foot
onto the gravel and grass, heat & cool,
she smiles at the source, something she can exist in whole,
absorb through her skin and hair, direct to the navel.

O

Most of the world is sky,
a mere crust of houses.
When a woman walks
she heals the scar
that should be healed, leaves
the others alone. On our streets
we paint large square letters.
The paint is smooth to the cheek.
Stop says the word. A woman
goes stalking clear across that O
and the day is carved up
and set in the navel of the horizon,
going down. At twilight
there are lips going around the foundation
of each house. The eyelashes
have just been mown down. The houses
look like convicts. Desire is a
large thing, but not large enough
to set them free. On our streets
we paint single words. The paint
is smooth to the cheek. The woman
wears faux leopard and candy
blue pumps. I wore out
a path to the river
long ago. Stop
says the word.
We aren't allowed.
We ain't being done
or soothed.

STEALING FIREWOOD

The way to steal firewood is
when your mom's in the hospital.
It doesn't work any other way. I tried,
just last week, because the wood was there
on the other side of the fence,
and everything went wrong.

Lucky I made it away. I didn't think.
I just drove, fast. I was so busy not thinking
the only way I knew I was getting close to town
was, the radio suddenly tuned in. I looked up
and there was the ocean, big like it usually is,
but a storm cloud had come down and covered the whole sky
except for one sliver near the water. That one sliver
of light reminded me of how stingy I am
with my buddies, not in a big way
like anyone could point to it, but they're
always buying me beers and giving me
ammunition, because they got it. Well, I
never got it, but my pockets aren't empty.

So, it was the ocean and the sky
being generous with something
like why couldn't my old man and my old
lady make something like that when they fight.
As long as they got to be fighting,
to at least not embarrass me.
My neighbor told me once she tried to commit
suicide by taking a whole bunch of pills.
She took the pills and everything, but
there was a knock at the door. She answered it.
An old couple had come to visit. She went
around bringing out cookies for them and making
tea, banging her head against the refrigerator
to stay awake. They stayed for hours. She sat
up on the edge of the couch nodding, and jerking
herself awake. By the time they left, the sleepiness had passed.

I used to think politeness in women like that
was pretty dumb. I still think it is.
We do some pretty stupid stuff and then it
goes and saves our lives. I forget these things.
I carry on conversations in my head with my buddies
all the time, things they wouldn't otherwise
know, and the next time I see them,
they're fine. It takes a lot of loneliness
to be like that. I can see that. I'm full
of other people—my grandfather, my uncle,
my old man, and Jerry Luck. I admire him.
He's almost not lonely. Soft. Just scared
sometimes. All these stupid things we do.
And then there's the army.

EUCHARIST

Digestion gets in the way of prime eating.
I could eat Congress for instance,
except they would digest and come out
as little pellets and grow manacles.
I could eat the moment of eclipse
and relive my own birth ride down
the tortured hypotenuse. I could
really fly, really sing, and all other moments
on airplanes, in dreams, at the lecture hall,
would be practice, what I did in a former
strangulation. Digestion means that
we surrender: hard shapes to soft shapes,
marriages to quiet mornings
when we count the full loneliness
of our fingers across the face in the mirror
tracing quicksilver intentions, imagining
we catch a glimpse of our
great grandmother's great joy
for a moment under a flowering dress
in the courtyard of a church
*

at someone else's wedding
or did we mistake eating
for what causes us to make
moral decisions and did we put a
pretty name to our rage
and did we dress it like doll's fire
before we hung the dolls on nooses
across the hallway, like I did at five,
duplicating *something*
while everything quiet in life
began to be sinister. As a young child
what didn't get said was adultery,
but grandma played cards a lot and I made toast
with butter melted by mysterious electricity.
I learned how to use
the invisible and how to mend
what is against the law
to be broken. And that we are digested
slowly, in shivers of pleasure
as we transit from one emotion
to another, through a system of harmonics
or typhoid. If we could make a lethal strain
of this happiness . . . but it's resistant,
elusive. Instead we have the criminal justice system,
and the tradition of Sunday Brunch
replacing church, voluptuary
of the crystal, croissant altar,
the biblical Sunday paper,
the long slow thought
carefully tended with coffee
which degrades into the sensual
or evolves
while all around us the street
emits cars
the longing emits a sequence of events
which lead
to joy, a plastic joy
useful
recyclable
✼

emoting. A joy
which digests us
even as we lean forward
into the breath
of the beloved.

HAWAI'IAN CEMENT

It's hard working in a cement factory. For one thing,
it's beautiful. But it's the kind of beauty which isn't
discussed. It's industrial, all right? Pastel white tanks,
but enormous, like monstrous virgins in the moonlight,
smooth, round, with spiral ladders winding around them,
and the stenciled letters are done in the same blue
that's the sky between clouds, and that long low barbed wire
fence that goes around it all like a wicked grin,
and then there's the smell, somewhere between dust
and what's history, the feeling you get standing
and looking down through generations. The dock workers strike.
Honolulu. 1938. My grandfather led the workers as they moved
forward over the docks to stop the scabs. Police opened up
on them with fire hoses, then tear gas, then guns full of buckshot.
The strikers didn't back off. They sat down.
Later, the police said they aimed for below the knee,
but how can you aim below the knee of someone
who's sitting cross-legged? Almost 50 of them ended up
in the hospital. Bert Nakano carried metal the rest of his life.
I run a fork lift on account of all that. I make decent
money, bring it home for my family. My grandfather's
father was Greek. He told me how sheep bells
are tuned to different musical modes so the sheep
moving through the landscape make melodies for the shepherd.
The Phrygian mode could be a working man's paradise.
You wonder why I smile so broadly in the morning when I hear
that fork lift backing up? It's those bells warning us to
keep back. It's my grandfather's voice rising up out of the
lava rock by Kailua Airport. It's the Phrygian labor union
*

anthem and it's why I would never admit
what beauty there could be. Why talk about what's not fancy?
There just comes a moment in your life when everything fits,
and if you don't know what I mean, it'll eat you
alive, that kind of beauty.

CINDERELLA II

FOR GARLON

Good, dark anger, the chocolate kind, the kind
spent at a gambling casino when love is—
Old, crazy anger, the best kind, the kind that moves
mountains when aimed, dangerous the possibility
of displacing the self when bitten—
Treacherous anger and seductive, wanting to mold
and bend the unmoldable, and then some. Gives power
over and destroys at the same time. The cars
on the road will all be crooked. Daylight will hang
in tatters. Walking down the road, the emasculated
self, the iron rod of grief striking footsteps
into earth. Trouble runs puddling
over the road. The grass wilts. The children see strangely.
I bend over and see my face distorted by water looking
back at me and I think: grief, you are a medication.
I measure myself against this crime and wake up tasting—
I had blood in my mouth, a whole spoonful, and my job
seemed to be carrying it to the fire intact without—
How did the dark stains get on my fingers where
has my throat been all night. Who made this mistake
making me—I smear lamp black across the gods and bend
ordinary at the sink gulping water. Contamination: the art
of concealing disrespect so well that you can taste
but not fight it. Ancestration: the act of poisoning one's forebears.
Quietude—the enormous suck of the wave before tidal pressure
forces it to cross itself. To have a child born of poison
is to spend the rest of one's days horribly awake.

NAMING HURRICANES

Immigration Office, San Francisco, 1996

You more American than me
because of still being an immigrant,
illegal, unlawful, waiting
like a clock hand, the inevitable
dignity of the hunted when the hunt
is conducted in English. When the hunt
stops, what makes us American
becomes slick:
it becomes more about
absence.
Freedom from things.
Freedom from each other
and from love.
We construct slow moments
behind glass and pretend
it's crazy, but it
makes that kind of morbid
sense of the schizophrenic:
vases in a flower.
Ordinary smoke,
extraordinary mouth.
Death without phone number.
My name is American and I can choose
whatever name I want. What happens
when naming breaks down? My father's name
after all, is only a counterpoint, the
falling tone, betraying a mother so large,
it took five generations to find enough
pieces of her. Now we are ordinary.
We would never think of emigrating.
Where would we go?

BLURRING

The problem is, we blur. At the moment
of crisis, the critical moment,
we blur. If we could just
open our eyes as the rope swing
makes its last precious ascent
and make something of our knees
and throat, arrange our happiness,
we could get married
every day. If I could only
forget my fear and look around
as I descend through pain,
betrayal, succulence,
but I blur, and then there is only
a cartoon-like frozen image
between the leap off and the
crack of the water's
surface. Perhaps all of life is out there
like a wild audience.

Tracy Porterfield

ESCARGOT

A snail
has plastered himself
to my window.
He moves
along
making
progress.

His fleshy antennae
pulse out
searching for lettuce
or rose petals.
He sucks along
with invisible feet,
finding only rosemary
and oregano.

Once, my mother unsealed
two snails mating
in her garden.
She held them up
to the light of the sun,
so I could see
the male's sex straining—
another antenna.

I was alarmed
by her fascinated smile.
She tossed
the garden intruders out
into separate galaxies
where objects are crunched
in the night.

My mother loves flowers
more than snails.

I see that my snail
has settled
for the rosemary.
I am thinking of
garlic and French bread
with lots of melted butter.

BLUE ROOM

I notice how the clouds
take up so much of the sky
and then there's
plenty of space left over.

Tonight the sun
hid behind
Mt. Tam
serving up rays
of soft pink and blushing peach,
kissing a few select and lucky
tips of clouds.

I thought:
A child's room should be
painted this way—
walls of powder blue
to give the child
that sense of limitless space
and pearly colored
puff clouds
for worlds and worlds
of cooing and dreaming.

BASED ON "VINEYARDS AT AUVERS" VINCENT VAN GOGH, 1890

Autumn vineyards
of blue harvested vines
lined by scattered blossoms
and the low rickety fences
indicating boundaries
for the wondering inhabitants
of white houses whose roofs are made of
dried orange grass.

Among the overgrown lawns
and ancient dirt roads
a stream runs somewhere.
It ribbons down from the purple mountains
past rabbit holes
and fawn trails
and the secret spaces
belonging to lovers
and to builders of tree forts
and to painters long gone
and to no one
but the tiny violet flowers with no names.

BODY THOUGHTS

The body longs for ecstasy
and the brain reasons.

Reason is an evil brute
within any pleasure dome.

For myself,
I am filled with gratitude
when I
come to
and the weight of my body
is supported by a cloud
✳

and the tip of my nose tingles
and breathing is rose-petal soft
and pleasurable as angora.

My body is invaded by hunger.
Hunger comes in colors of orange and pepto pink.
It rakes the insides
and takes the breath away.
It saps juice from the muscles
and even the brain.
Hunger is a beast that pushes at my back
as I walk away from whatever I'm doing
to hunt for food.

My body reveals histories.

Your body is as smooth
as the bright and graceful
succulent
that arches
in my terra cotta pot.

But what could be holier
than the spacious brow?
Possibly the two lines
that connect the nose and the upper lip
where an angel pinched
his seal
before the great send-off.

God had mercy
when he molded the brow.
I have not seen one yet
that wasn't exquisite
as fresh blown hillocks of sand.

It's almost painful to watch a sleeping brow,
poised in dream land
inviting a touch
which would only break the spell
and cause two slits to open
and reveal orbs full of light
startled and questioning as eyes of babes.

CHRISTMAS

The sun moves low on the horizon
dead branches reach out into cold empty spaces
grey and startled by their own death.

It is Christmas time again.
I am busy with things I have to do.
I'm sitting at my desk
poised, pen in hand
and gazing out the window
at the mossy trunks of trees.
I'm listening for the magical message
that the boisterous, leather-jacketed ravens will surely bring.

I go for a walk.
Icy, grey mist gives over to piercing rays of light.
I step gingerly through a carpet of wet bay leaves
their spicy scent probes me
with memories of Christmas past,
pine needles, cranberries, ribbons and bows.

And then the white line
of a jet streaking across the perfect blue sky
snaps my head around.

The image has always been your private hello
and forever brings me back to what's at hand.

I won't be seeing you this Christmas.
You will only be a white streak
across the sky,
a single glove lying in the road,
a red Ninja motorcycle
or any of the senseless symbols
I clutch onto
in homage to you
my little brother.

Helen Reynolds

UNTITLED

Evening cool—
    crystal arch from the hand-held hose
      the hummingbird drinks

                        Afternoon sunlight—
                          goldfinch flits from the laurel
                            a yellow leaf falls

The bedside jot—
    my midnight masterpiece
      isn't so hot

                        Over a stone wall
                          acacia heavy with spring
                            gild a tombstone

In my cupped hand
    the stunned hummingbird is—
      gone

                        jarring fall jelly—
                          the mother-in-law eyes
                            the July bride's belly

Summer dusk—
    in the homing cows moo
      her rounded udder

Opening—closing
   wings of the new butterfly
      measure my breathing

                    Break in the clouds—
                       rain-drenched hummingbird
                          bursts into flame

Day in day out
   sexual harassment—
      the old rooster

                    Distant gull cry—
                       the whale's misty fountain
                          returns to the sea

Lingering dust—
   the flagman fans himself
      with his stop-sign

                    Wine on the warm air—
                       in sun-mottled shade
                          mangoes and maggots

Mounding clouds—
   a white egret lights
      on a grazing horse

Stephanie MacLean

ABOUT ROBERT PENN WARREN

Little Bobby drooled blissfully
and slept the sleep of old men.
In the hammock where Nurse rocked him,
he dozed and smiled.
The sun zoomed into his eye
and Bobby's baby eye zoomed back and saw the Woman looming
above him.
He saw the Woman's marcelled hair:
he inhaled her faint scent
of glycerin and rosewater.
The Woman's arms lifted him up into the world.
The sky made him dizzy.

Bobby wandered by the water;
the river, dank and fecund,
rousing him from the sleep of youth,
filling him with questionings he could not name.
He didn't talk much, burning with words.

He followed the river, streaming with tiny worlds,
clots caught full and complete,
isolated by a wrong-ended telescope,
the child's eye.

The pliant river oozed life.
Bobby squeezed river slime
between his toes
and slapped the cooling mud with his feet.
He observed the skeeter bugs and water dogs,
skittering newts and fat beetles
with shining undersides and backs,
frescoed with pictures he could never hope to paint.

Mother and Papa all propelling him towards that moment—
Self and his meeting with love, first love,
*

downy with fine cornsilk—
hairpins slithered from her hair, she rustled
when she walked, starched and crisp and soft all at once,
her voice murmuring like a hesitant breeze.
He swooned to know her and told no one,
not even himself.

In love and lust, the promise of experience overshadowed him;
he held it in his mouth
like sweet wine he tasted,
but could not swallow.
Confusion stirred his groin and
sweat gathered at the back of his neck,
a sign for all to see.

Bobby wondered about the silence
he saw in the ponds
on late summer afternoons
when every thing was asleep.
He wandered on full moon nights
when the hot, sticky air like syrup
suffocated him and he drove
with the girl in search of cool
and a private place to try to touch her.
He had to know another to know himself.

Silently assenting, nature saying yes yes yes to life
and no one listening,
people afraid to listen.
Up in their mansions and down
in their hovels and boardinghouses,
spooning off that last bit of pie,
lighting fine cigars on their porches,
whimpering the dead dream into damp pillows.

Robert thought if we knew our fate
we'd never dare to dream it.

He did not deny himself, the poet,
love of words and mean sights,
storyteller in search of a story.
*

He saw it all and all had equal weight—
the bleating lamb,
the dozing bee,
sweaty men, emerging from blue smoke of manly deliberation,
and women with chapped, reddened hands,
bending over eternal sinks of dishwater,
making the world clean.

He saw people running,
silly as skeeter bugs, he thought,
running with no discernible direction, banging heads, coupling accidentally.
He saw men whose palms were up and smooth,
but turn the hand down,
topside was a map of country roads:
What's wrong with these people, he asked,
who planted painted rocks in astroturf garnished with plastic flamingos?
Why does growing up in the world mean growing away from it?

Perfumed and humid, the day is
heavy as Aunt Erma's biscuits.
Sun gives him a headache
like bourbon or a broken heart;
he takes comfort inside the house, filling the suitcase
with sheaves of spidery, penciled traceries;
later, inked papers, then typewritten.
He looks at the welcoming blank sheet and smiles.
To know a truth is to write the truth,
for the telling of it gives us hope.

Robert grew old and feathers sprouted from his hair.
The ringlets gave him a perpetually
boyish look, peeved and curious.
Though parts of him were slack,
his eyes were ageless.

He married late in life,
he was fond of telling,
but blossomed early.

Wind fretted the leaves
as he sat in the dappled shade.
*

Now seeing life without the veil,
musing on what Heraclitus said:
". . . you can't step into the same river twice."
Glancing down, those ageless eyes
followed silver snail trails.
Snails know where they're going, he thought.

Dozing in the twilight
about the time fireflies appear;
see that battered suitcase, scuffed leather,
one strap flaccid, loosened from its buckles,
brass fittings want polishing, still upright and sturdy,

the paper swells contain his boyhood
and its wealth of knowledge,
his observation of life,
truncated by his yearning for home,
a repository, the place to be.
He saw himself wading
through life from boy to man
with river grasses
still clinging to his ankles.

Pursuit of truth, he noted,
is the only journey worth taking.

Might be another baby in the hammock now
Nurse comes to fetch,
descended from Bobby's blood.

Thighs spilling like jelly
where once they were hard as logs,
Woman comes ramming at his hips;
his eyes dissolve in stars.

Patricia O'Donnell

L e o n a

Leona,
being quite old,
had a high regard for life
and did not weed her garden
anymore.

e n t h u s i a s m

everything i do
i want to do forever!
and then,
oh god,
will i be doing THIS forever?

g o o d b y e

autumn leaves,
little gondolas of red and gold,
sit lightly on the water

say goodbye to summer

h i r o s h i m a

snow falls
and moon rises
cranes dance in white light

sweet night
cranes sleep

moon wanes
and dawn comes
temple shakes, stones fall down

cranes dance in red blaze
all worship new master

Fionna Perkins

CHOICE

For him an easy death,
legs buckling, body going limp
an instant after the injection.
Weeks of indecision ended
by the veterinarian's thrust
of a needle to his heart.

When is the moment
to ask the mercy killing
for an old and faithful friend,
when he whimpers,
tries to rise and legs collapse?

I said *it's time*,
but how could I be sure?
His own one life, like ours,
was all he had.
In pain, failing, did he want
another hour, another day?

Vacillating, I read of parents
whose doomed baby doctors
could have kept alive a few days,
a few weeks. They chose to let
her go, together holding their
joined lives her last hours.

Whether an old dog, new life
forming, a fatally-impaired infant,
saying yes to death
claims two, the one that goes,
the one that stays. We keep
private anniversaries, we women.
Signing the paper, I died a little,
die again at each remembering.

AS THE CIRCLE EMPTIES

Still with me
through years of absence,
they appear unsummoned
to sit and visit
in rooms
they never knew.

I see their faces,
gestures, lips moving,
these interlopers
so casually at home
who make no sound.

The abiding grief,
they cannot hear
or speak aloud
nor can we ever
touch again.

ALERT!

Twice at early light
a raven flew by my window,
raucous cries jolting

me awake to fear of
omens and sudden demise,
though hardly premature,

given that I was here
for the third decade of a
century now in its ninth,

affording me many long,
traumatic and miraculous
years to contemplate,

if looking backward—having
lived them—but seeing ahead,
they seem no time at all,

as if I'd just stepped off
an airplane or down from a bus,
my bags still packed.

Joan Rosen

COMPTCHE CABIN CONCERTO

The hum and drone of the old Coldspot, a solid cello tone.
    The shudder when she shuts off.
The rhythmic thwack, thud of chopping wood.
    A percussive echo'd note.
Bleets of sheep, deep and occasional—like tympany drums.
The swoosh and whirr, hustle and rustle of the wind playing leaves softly.
    Poplar and redwood, willow and fir.
The clop, clop of a horse plodding along the roadway,
    horseshoes striking a two-step.
The flutes come on—robins and larks; the trumpets are the crows.
    The jays a shrill refrain.
The river runs through here. Soft harp music in the summer.
Woodwinds play: chickens crow and duck as clarinets.
    A distant mooing becomes a bassoon.
Hush now. You can almost hear the fog rise . . . . . . before a logging
    truck rumbles through and carries the silence away.

RAIN GAUGE

Rain Gauge. How it draws me to it.
The deepness of its pool, the lyric of its cascade
The lushness of its setting, yet just below the road grade.

Pickups and lumber trucks whizz by
While the pond lies hidden in huckleberry and hazelnut
Protected by poison oak, granite, and redwoods;
Rimmed by tigerlilies, dainty alum
Carpeted by mosses, ferns and liverwort
Soft, feminine, welcoming and icy cold!

"Rain Gauge" they call it—on the Albion River
Where there are mechanisms to measure stream flow for the salmon runs.
✿

Now disengaged. A remnant. Like the salmon . . .
But the pool's beauty defies use and abuse,
Storms and draught, logging and roadwork.
Stable and serene it remains a grotto that gives us hope.

Shauna Smith

UNTITLED

We struggle against each other
Rocks trapped in swampy rivers
Vying for position.

Mud covers us
Turns clear blue water
Opaque.

Let us not work so hard,
Further down, the river is deep,
There is clarity and coolness
And room for us all.

UNTITLED

You can't fight inertia,
A crab stuck on a dry rock
After the tide has gone down.

What can be done?
A time to rest,
Draw nourishment
        from banked seaweed,
Lie quiet in the sun.

Be a silent, brittle sculpture,
Collecting passive power,
Waiting for the water's return.

TWELVE

My daughter is twelve
And does she know it.

"I can remember my *own*
        headgear, Mother,
Fix your hair, Mother,
You don't love me,
I don't fit in this family, Mother."

And her words roll back and forth
Like the ocean's drone.

"I am sorry," I say,
"I won't nag,
I'll fix my hair,
I do love you, and
Of course you belong . . . "

My daughter rolls her eyes scornfully,
As only twelve year olds can do.

I cannot stop it:
Uncontrollably I laugh
Then gently draw her close;
She cannot help it:
She yields to my touch,

And our words are silenced
In the ocean's roar.

Judy Summers

LEARNING TO BE A BOY, NOT FOR MY FATHER BUT FOR ME

My mother told me, "your father wasn't disappointed that you weren't a boy,"
I knew she lied.
Or did she refer to the well-known fact that he did care that my sister Beth was not
    a boy?
"Bethie Boy" was my sister's nickname,
She was loud; she was insistent.
He never liked her.
And for a long time, neither did I.
Not a boy.
It's strange to grow up in the stifled air of not.
The first time a boy showed me a penis I was 6 and he was 3.
I was horrified.
Not by the flabby, pink thing he presented, but by the aplomb of its owner.
At 3 so certain he possessed a jewel between his short legs.
And liked me enough to show it off.
I ran from the room.
I did not have the jewel.
I never asked myself why would I want something I thought so ugly.
I have turned myself inside out being a nice girl.
The only kind of girl who could live in the stifled air of not.
Nice is not enough to live on.
I am so many years into my life.
To let this in and breathe it out is both a relief and a revelation.
Many steps are taken just to let go.

Suzanne Byerley

UNTRUSTING

Driving home
I see
ahead of me
a curved ancient
tilt up the road
like a toddler
bowlegged
not moving fast
but moving.

Thirty feet beyond
a black dog lies
in his path.

I pass,
slow,
watch in the mirror
breathless,
the man
drawing nearer,
eighty
ninety
perhaps God,
the dog planted there
the man slowing
slowing
leaning
offering his hand
I do not breathe
until
my mirror
overflows
with the motion
of the black broom
sweeping the road
with joy.

THREE FROM OCTOBER IN THIS CORNER

10/3

Here it is
October
and the
maple above me
still dark green.
A single rust-streaked
drifter lands
beside me,
first of thousands.
In Ohio
we pushed
through millions
from Lee Road to
what was
the name of
that street
I knew like
my own name?
Never mind.
The quail are
especially noisy.
I wonder
why their wings
make so much
more racket
than the
chickadee's,
why there is
infinite life
on this
tiny
ball,
why we can't find
other live ones.
It's lonely here
*

acting as if we
knew what the hell
we're up to
when
we're all infants
at it.
One morning
day won't dawn
as bright
and we
will
slowly
freeze
or it
will dawn
too bright
and we
will
slowly
fry.
Then
who will
echo,
listen,
who then
will attend
to the relative
loudness
of bird wings,
the gradations
of leaf hue
in October?
Goodbye
October.
I'm saying it
in advance
while Spike
*

under the
still-green leaves
tries to eject
a hair ball,
a need
more immediate
than discovering our
neighbors
in the universe.

10/24
Finally
the maple
reddens,
the skinny
birch begins
to yellow,
dahlia leaves
are rags.
A buzzing
summons me.
A trapped fly?
Maybe just
my brain,
a variation
on tinnitus
so noisy
of late,
a thought
trying to
escape like
steam,
a cry
forced through
a synapse
toward
space,
*

a plea,
almost
indiscernible,
entirely
inadequate,
for more
time.

10/31
The tree has turned.
Wet gold leaves
against dark
green.
Everything here is
green
except
once a year
this brilliant intruder.
I towel off a chair,
green,
and I remember now
why I wanted
the furniture
painted yellow—
to hold out hope
for this one
gold week
out of the
deep
green
year.
If I liked
gold so much
I could have
stayed in Ohio.
I read
more Hawking
*

this morning
explaining
how minute
we are
how flimsy
on the finger
of the universe.
In the paper
Turkey/Greece
IRA/Ireland
Israel/Palestine:
squabbles in the
whisker corner
of the galaxy
conspire
to give
the illusion
of firm
where
there is
no firm.
Wealthy
ill
saintly
ignorant
all huddle
confidently
where someday
there will
be nothing.
I wish for
a minute
we could
experience
the speed
at which
we rocket.
It might
have an impact
*

on negotiations,
open momentarily
an eye to
misery,
shock the shit
out of
our arrogant
star spangled
blindness.

No wonder
we cherish
the animals,
prefer the
calling of
the birds.
The soft chrk
of crow
just beyond
those trees.
The higher pitch
responding,
the low vibration
moving.

I would go.
I would
answer
that purr
of call.

Lydia Rand

MY MOTHER'S SPECTER

Today I am alone again roaming the Fall countryside
spiked with sunflower stalks left over from recent harvest.
As I walk across turned up fields, across fallow lands
and reach the drenched vineyards holding on to their grapes,
I remember the dream of rivers flowing from my mother's body to mine.

I pick fossils from deep furrows, I listen to the song of the rook,
and my mother's specter is here by my side,
leaving on the darkening sky a place paler than the rest.
"Autumn has turned up what was buried deep," she says in her voiceless way.
Pointing towards the wind—a warm surprise to the skin—she accuses
the gentle ferocity herding threatening clouds and plotting the dreary season.

"See how it was for me, all those winters alone, under cold's spell,
without sun, without you, my daughter, only blizzards and storms
and death's prospect banging on my door.
Only one daughter who left me by myself to die a lonely death
in unfriendly regions, far from my homeland.
Disregarding my cautions, she joined sorcerers in their houses of games
and rode lonely winds to gather up lost twins.

"Here, in this garden of France, after crops are gathered
and hunting is over, all doors are shut tight; there is no longer room
for human compassion. The lonely can die alone, they are shaped
by their fears, their pain the result of too much indulging.
Stay away from them, their dis-ease is catching.
No my daughter, I won't have you roam the misty countryside
looking for forgiveness. Love is the flower of the beaten path
and anyone who cares to bend can find it.

"There you go again,
on the traces of faded flowers and lost men's poetry.
Entering their picture you become
that young girl with a small head and huge body
—you know the one—she holds a withered bouquet in her lap.
*

It frightens me to find you making your way on this trail of fugitive impressions.
The mirror holding your twin is now broken. I cut myself on its edges.
My faint heart, stuck on survival mode, failed to soar,
and my destiny fell short of wisdom
in spheres where dark entities prey on you.

"I saw them staring at you in your darkened room,
I saw them dense and muscular, curling around your chest on moonless nights.
Do you remember, soon after I died,
when the psychic octopus prevented your journeying spirit
from re-entering the shelter of your deserted body?
Do you remember how your life force leaked into the mouth of the beast?
You guessed right. I was the one who tore the monster off your chest.

"Go home now, my daughter. Build yourself a fire.
This winter doesn't promise another spring. You will have to make your own.
Forget your boy cousin, forget your father's tribe,
the high cheek bones, the Italian houses made of stone.
Sunflowers are withered. Don't you know? That is what killed Van Gogh.
Come, sit with me by the fire.
Give up poets, sorcerers and those failed magicians, the philosophers.
Turn on the light and sing to me, begin the weaving, the embroidery, the knitting.
Work on the cloth of the ordinary. I have been so lonely, ever since you left me."

THE BREAK

TO ELLA

There was a truce,
a break in the gloomy curtain of rain,
an hour or two of this slanted light,
lifting people and things out of solidity
and into simple clarity,
a space where each second
the world was created anew . . .
And every moment of self
showered with the golden manna of soul
unfolded,
in this place beyond memory your mother was so familiar with
*

in the last years of her life.
Do you remember that we once dwelled there together?

There you stood, your family and your rabbi
stretching on each side of you like wings
with which you caught the life current and glided
as an eagle,
over the great plains of your ancestry.
In the shimmering flow of forebears you surveyed,
your mother's life at times
was like the fearful prey going against current
you might have caught.
But you had compassion,
and the burden of rain flew away from us.

Your mother was my mother, Ella, as I shed a tear with you.
It was my mother they lowered into the ground,
and Lillia's,
and all the mothers I hadn't taken the time to sit with
in quietness
or write poems about.
My mother inspired me most once she was dead.
There was such youthful neglect in my impatient soul,
and the stallion of my heart kept devouring the miles ahead
forgetting the life right under its hooves.
I cried for all the mothers, Lillia's, yours and mine,
and those others making a big circle above our own,
and shedding all those tears for their own mothers,
and the mothers of the mothers.
We are the mothers now,
there is no one ahead shielding us from death's inquisition.

I once fell in an ancestral well.
Looking too deep and too long into my baby girl's blue eyes
I joined the chain of women
reaching for more women,
reaching for truth,
while washing away the sins of the fathers.

And there, in the slanted light, we all went down into that well.
Breaking open our containers we poured out of our habitual form
*

and merged together into one slow stream.

You had invited us Ella, to fly with you in this perfect light,
with this perfect love in our heart,
at this perfect moment in time,
in this place in which we could do nothing but the right thing.

The blessings of a winter day.

SHE WHO TAKES HER LIFE IS ALWAYS WAITING

She was a writer.
She hated her mother.
She loved men way too much.

She read us one of her stories about a little green chair
that stood empty in front of her
as she talked,
endlessly,
from thousands of miles away,
to her best friend,
on the telephone,
week after week,
year after year,
talked about herself,
about the new bastard that ran her life,
about the hurt, the dramas and disappointments,
about her loneliness.
Across from her, the patient little green chair
stood through it all, trying to reach out,
but she was so wrapped in her misery, she never even noticed.

No one ever pointed out the way out of her dungeon,
no one showed her how to win the heart of the prince,
and the lips that joined hers in a kiss were only illusions.
She learned that rescuers and heroes never pan out,
and life doesn't keep its promises.

The little green chair stood there,
waiting to be sat on and recognized,
waiting to be given a chance to exist,
but there was only space for one need in the tiny room.

Years after she had given away the little green chair,
she remembered it as a dear friend she had passed by and missed,
just as she recalled us,
her two noctambulist friends,
long after we were gone,
enrolling us in her story, but never giving us a voice.

The story was about three chairs facing each other
like on the night we parted.
The three of us had walked on moonlit nights and sat there to rest;
now the chairs waited for us to come back,
resume our nocturnal conversations.

She only could love whoever kept her waiting.
When we were with her, she remembered
her absent friend at the other end of the line,
always listening,
and the chair,
always waiting;
and she remembered us when we were gone.

She gave us what she could,
—a song by her favorite singer, Violetta Parra,
a country, Argentina—
then she waited for things to get better.
But they didn't.
So she slipped away in a winter dream,
just like Violetta
who thanked life and swallowed her death,
washing it down with Tequila
and sitting on a chair,
waiting.

THE VOICE

She has no voice.
She wants to scream for help
but not a sound will come out.
Her soul has been stolen.
A dense entity sits black on the area that was her chest, sucking it out.
She struggles to recover the space once occupied by her body,
but when her voice finally slips back into her throat
she screams "This is not my voice."

She'd worked hard to find that voice.
In her early twenties she wrote pages after pages,
using words to dig a tunnel for that voice to come through.
In her thirties, she cleaned up her psyche, writing more than ever to expel
the voices that bewitched her ever since birth.
In her forties she was discouraged and lonely,
how could she ever get to that voice?
The voice was calling her from over the hills, from the other side of things,
it echoed hers but it was not it,
sometimes she heard it right in her ear, as a tender whisper.
In her deepest silence the voice was there,
when nothing was moving, in the dead of night
the voice was there,
but when she tried to grasp it,
it ducked.
In her fifties she heard the voice as a ringing that twisted her body
into an impossible sound.
Following the guidance of the voice,
she labored to move it through the clogged channel,
push it out, push it out . . .
And it rose loud and clear, a magnificent singing voice,
a brand new voice,
without ancestry, without background or culture,
a unique voice,
her own voice.

She called it *Ma Voix*,
and realized that the word also meant my path,
and the writing,
✻

which was the path her voice borrowed
was acclaimed as original, praised as universal . . .
Then everyone began to want to change the voice.

To keep its popularity,
the voice had to represent the tendency of the moment,
deal with the latest issues,
the current cultural neurosis,
it must ridicule the national psychosis.

She went back into silence, began dreaming again.

Like Saint Francis
when he was most confused and lonely, most empty,
she heard the voice of the father
demanding that Francis rebuild the church.
And Francis took it literally,
—stone by stone, this little church in Assisi—
he gave up his rich robes, became a mason, a pauper.

Like Rasputin when he was most humiliated and angry,
she heard the voice of the mother
in the utter silence after rage.
The mother's voice told him to save the future king.
He took it literally, embracing the fairy tale
and presenting himself at the palace
to heal the dying boy who was heir to the kingdom.
He gave up his wretched rags and put on the princely garbs.

Like Joan and Bernadette she heard the voices,
mother, father, sisters and sons,
but where, she questioned,
is the voice that no longer doubts,
the fearless voice moving the inner,
guiding the outer,
where is the voice that rises
to occupy the infinite space of body,
setting in motion the divine inspiration in all worldly things,
trading cloth or building churches,
keeping house or healing kings.

Catherine Potenza

WALKING HOME

walking home
wondering how to make love
more than heart ache

summer street market sweet peas please
gladiola glories
red ripe tomato cheek farm boys
quoting their father's voice

an old woman arguing about taste

love was never boring
another person

washing your mouth with wine
secrets in bottles crossing the ocean
flotsam of heartache
closets of approved threads
bald heads in airports
holding together in urinals
birds shattered in jet engines
newspapers exposing
hotel beds
very shy young man
seeking older woman

the comet in the night sky
comes to the roof top

a new moon swells
opposite a single star

the young man loses his voice

it's quiet

dark and seeming nothing
countless stars
almost sound
fall to the ground
down the dark sky to sea

passion crashes like a freak wave
all falls naked and stranded on shore
still alive

STARS FALL

Stars fall all the way to the ground
A miniature skyline of the village
appears at the end of the road
curving forest and coast
The darkness and quiet
vast and still

after city lights
home
don't even try to understand

Stars fall all the way to the ground
ground, sound, under sea wind
waving grasses round women's hips
fresh deep dark winter earth
greeting their nostrils

the buoys breathe
in the darkness
home in bed

a star
stars over a dark sea
a leftover slice of moon

lights out
dark roofs weigh on tall windowless walls
*

mists of pale white between dark hills
thrills of softness, still and silent

sadness

seen in the joker's queen
streets of quiet moving crowds
soft and safe and fresh
like a mother
silence on squares
sitting on trams
staring still
without looking
strangers acknowledge
sadness is normal
no shame
on moravian trams

distant thunder, claps of lightning
quiet rooms, sudden cuts of light
horrible roars of clouds
close rain pour of water
pounds walls

THE SHORE

The shore and the sea
a wild welcome expanse
a surreal scene
slow motion glance
a small clan of sea worshippers
come for service
a warm grey unsunday
hidden below cool clouds
in silver blue nature
humming birds mate
snails ooze elusive refuse

The shore and the sea
the wide empty sand
escapes the claustrophobic
familiar chores the shore ignores
swallowed into blue ocean sky
white wave whispers
in the ears
fresh kisses on the face

The shore and the sea
naked ladies grace
narrow single high
purple vulva stems
bloom bad taste pink
in wild fields of straw gold

proffer purple berries
the ripe sweet come easily
to the fingers
gather in clusters
die quickly
to expansive grey mould
unless eaten fresh

snap dragons velvet
humming birds hover
taste fuchsia tongues
bees explore California poppies
a cat naps

on cliffs sculpt stone giants
reflecting in still clear pools
intimate interiors at low tide
exposed

LAST WALTZES

Last waltzes
such a wet fog falls
the ground is dark
the sky light white
the wet warm still chill
of the invisible and obscure
ocean

the crash of glass trash shatters
the Friday morning outside
sleeping bodies in beds
floating awake behind walls
and through windows
of pitched roof salt box houses
lining streets a few walk early
alone, some with styrofoam cups,
some with newspapers,
some from the same bed

Will it last?
Many last.

We laugh, weep, deep wells still
fresh, vital, wild, natural
wells of smiles, of well yesses
wells guesses, kisses, misses

whispers of kisses in the ear
wells of wishes, best, only
well wishes and fondest dreams

lies in disguise
fantasies hidden
feelings forbidden

rush to work

press
swirling, spiraling
✳

resistance and longing
driving deep
dread and desire

wells of oil
wells of force
wells of weapons
wells of wounds
wells of pain

HEIDER FIELD

Heider field
great yield the square in the village is
a field of straw spun gold in summer
that flowers a woman's hips in spring
a skirt of wild blooming to seed
and cut to the ground safe from fire

empty and wild
save the foot-worn path
crossing the open space
and breath of nature
found frightened midst
business in a village
few are born
many came alone

Father Time and the Maiden
carved in virgin redwood
stand on the highest rooftop
high above the people below
entering the temple door
to speak to tellers behind bars
lining little windows
guarding money

ABALONE

"It's blue outside!" she said
and went to bed
after a downpour

she leaves her music
her voice
a cup of tea
choice olive oil
fresh produce
generosity

Birds chirp, intermittently dogs bark
The ocean breathes, wind through leaves
whispers kisses

Gold pours over falling fuchsias
Gold California poppies alight

Light paints the garden sculpture
An angel bathes its feet

Birds come to bathe
Splashing fountains of water wings

A goddess in the spectrum
stands on the mountain
shoulders shawled
head bent forward
looking down

A dragon floats on a cloud carpet
sheltering her body
bending gently forward
within dignity

The heavens are colored
rose and blue green
the scene in a shell
of Abalone
the Indians wore
to ward off sadness

MENDOCINO WEATHER

Earth turns
Horizons burn
Witches at stake
Stalk the streets
And curl in antique chairs

Risen from the river's cleft
The moon combs light
Through unmown tresses
Tangled round wild rose buds
Sharing limbs
With aging blooms
that do not die unwitnessed

Flaming oak perfumes
Dove breasted sky

From beyond a hundred years
Weatherbeaten Mendocino faces
Stars and stories
Listening to the mulling throngs
Of life's beginnings
Gather round the buoys

Conceived in the image and likeness
The season is present
And ever will be

Sun rises
To rose petal skies
Virgin vapours lift
From chartreuse meadows
Where the Milky Way
in countless crystal balls
falls and lights
on grass and leaves
foretelling
Day

ruth weiss

JUNE 23rd, 1977
ANNA AKHMATOVA

today is your birthday
tomorrow is mine
it's '77
I'll be 49

at 77 you went
vowing never to return

does it matter
because you are a poet
your father denied you?

does it matter
because you are a poet
your country denied you?

you chose another name
but would not choose another place

at threat of death
you wrote it down
you tore it up
till each word meant
indelibled into memory

the MUSE chooses
and does not let go

it does not matter
it is just matter
the meaning is clear
the word lives on . . .

LISTEN PAPA

the fog parts
clears around the full moon
eye in the night sky
a pearl, a pupil bright
PAPA bright pupil
at 80 still taking courses
a photo of you at the xerox machine
the oldest student in school
in turlock california
where you finally found the roots
to end this lifetime in 1984

this full-moon night
celebrates your 100th anniversary
july 19th 1997
PAPA — crab-cancer sign
like me your daughter
your only offspring

roots stretched to hungary
to transylvania
the bow across the gypsy violin
haunts its centuries of wandering

this full-moon night in big sur 1997
where 40 years before
i stayed & healed
cut my feet on rocks to reach the sea
cut my cord dependent on cities
returning to the city
knew i'd widened my horizon

a century since you were born
13 years after your death
i write you

PAPA you would not ever listen
to a single word i said
can you hear me now

MOTHER'S DAY 1997

MUTTI you said you never learned to laugh
that's why you married PAPA
who did & loud & often after
his laughter would rebound
even after he left us in 1984

you said PAPA is calling me
went through THE GOLDEN DOOR in 1985 at 85
a year to the day on the jewish calendar
your middle name ZLATA
gold in yugoslav
your golden voice a gift to me

spider-woman spins
the sun turns the threads to gold
they sing in the wind

WENDY

WENDY is her own grandmother.   she makes a grandmother
doll.   just so people can tell them apart, but the doll
is a part of herself.   and bigger than she is WENDY
is tiny.   with a grin that circles the earth. and easy
tears.   that keep her fluid on the path.   as she travels
with her grandmother on her back.

who else could tell me how to make mashed potatoes.   and
walk soft.   on the hard road ahead.

ALene

the open window.   the lace curtain is moving.   the lace
curtain is moving.   that is why i moved here ALene sez.

she is sitting by the open window.   she is the open
window.   she is the curtain moving.

it is an inviting. this lace curtain moving. in the
open window.

and they arrive. one by one. to look through the lace
curtain. that goes deeper than a mirror. that goes
further than a mirror.

and one by one they bring back the image. and carry it
with them. away.

ALene looks at the stars, and bursts out laughing.

ELAINE

ELAINE in the elfin forest. knee-high in cypress.
her hand on a limb. her face in a flower. her
footprint that only the deer can tell.

the clay bowl she just made. under the huckleberries.
filling with huckleberries. dropping on their own.

ELAINE is looking up. pie in the sky she sez. her
voice tuning a spiderweb glistening in the sun.

FLAME

MOTHER EARTH kisses her bare foot. one foot then the
other. one foot then the other. as she walks through
the forest.

she faces to the east.
she faces to the west.
she faces to the south.
she faces to the north.

and thanks MOTHER EARTH for the gift from the trees.
to make fire-wood. to keep the flame alive. to make
human dwellings warm.

at her college graduation she painted her feet. to
simulate shoes. and walked bare-foot to her graduation:

now she leaves the working of wood.

goes to another graduation.

lifts her voice in all directions.

where she faces her pain. to learn the source of
the flame. to keep the flame alive.

she faces to the east.

YELL OW ! YELL WOW!

the sun is rising. on yet another day,

who'd have thunk it!

CAROL

CAROL is stirring her stew. in goes a shamrock.
in goes a shell. in goes a feather. in goes a truck.
the size of a thimble.

come look she sez. as she stirs the stew.   adding a
bit of this & a bit of that.

and yes there is a house. and the walk that goes to
it. the walk that brings all her friends & lovers
inside.

i guess i'm packed up & on my way she sez & picks up
the kettle. the kitten she saved from a dumpster
tucked under her arm.

BONNIE

it's five past the meridian hour.   you're late BONNIE sez.
we have to be back in time.

we enter her trailer.

but today it's a plane.   a two-seater with one propeller.
it's all a matter of balance.   one propeller.   two seats
for three.

her hands are on the controls.   in & out of the clouds.

her hands touch points on the meridian.   the great circle
of the earth passing through the poles.   the great circle
of the celestial sphere.   the great circle of the
human body.

And we land.   on a great stump of a redwood.   a great-
great-great-grandmother of a redwood.

this is the tree where he was given to be shaman.

this is the tree where he married.
this is the tree where he was i BONNIE sez.
the tree is gone. but the spirit lives on.
it doesn't hurt so much once you know that.

and out we go.   and touch the bark.   and feel
the circle around the stump.   the great circle of
the earth passing through the poles.   the great
circle of the celestial sphere.   the great circle
of the human body.

and out we go.   to a grove of redwood dancing,
limbs out every which-way.   through billowing
gauze of fog.   a wave crashes.   and again.

and then we're off.   and back again.   and oh do
we feel great.   the whole body.   the body whole.

we're back in time BONNIE sez.   flying is to see
how big the earth is.   and how small.

Jenny Gealey

CHILD'S WHEEL

I was a whisper
conceived in the golden time
  Summer
     turning
        to
           Fall
And mountains, the only ones
           silent enough
       heard me mumbling songs
   in my first unborn moment
But in this deep basin
    between Earth's rocky fingers
I could not stay long
   Fall
      to
         Winter
        to
           Spring

The next chapter begins
   in a hospital bed
touched by the ocean breath
   born in the emerald time
     Spring turning
     to Summer
Kelp castles and
   driftwood fortresses
heard my songs bounce off cliffs
   and ripple the ocean

And Summer
     to
         Fall
       to
           Spring
          to
             Summer again

7 times until I returned
    to the mountains

In a blink
    I had grown my own
        eyes
    my own
        voice
and to rock peaks
    and cradles
I returned
    and returned
Summer to
    Fall to
        Winter

Where an icy wind
    stole my songs
made me afraid
    to raise my voice

And now the power
    of that speck of child
against jutting peaks
    returns with the hail
        rides the winds
           of midnight
    saturates me with
        the rain
Child of salt water
    and rock
words now lost
    in thunder

MOUNTAIN AWAKENING

moonrise twice tonight
first a ripple in the lake
a giant firefly
drowning
then peeking shyly
over craggy rock
and snowbanks
white spotlight
scaring the stars away
making clouds
white feathers
we are tiny now
drowning in its splendor

UNTITLED

sitting with my back
to the unknown
facing out from my cave
I watch the outside
afraid to go inside
afraid to look behind
knowing only the beauty
that turns the water to glass
the power
that churns the waves
the afterglow of sunlight
the sky stained orange as
its mother dies again
each rock a survivor
each pebble of sand a reminder
my handprints scars
prism perfect
too easy to break

ABOUT THE POETS

Zomala Abell was born in Boston Mass. in 1939 and moved to Albion in 1968. She lived communally for 20 years, taught at an alternative school for 20 years, delivered babies and assisted deaths. Her roles have included traveler, meditator, lesbian, Jew, mother, grand-mother, joker, political activist, poet and explorer of inner space. At this time she is grateful to have no idea as to who she is.

Marilyn Alexander, after living most of her life in the desert, raising children, teaching gifted classes in writing and literature, and owning an educational publishing company, trans-planted herself to the edge of the ocean, where the pace is slower, cooler and greener. Now she has lots of time to read and write, and has started a small editing business.

Jane Lee Harris Austin became a northern Californian in 1986. She delights in returning to her mid-western roots to visit her three children and their families in Indiana, Michigan and the rocky slopes of Colorado. She also loves returning home to this birthing valley in the redwoods nestled next to the healing springs. Her master's thesis was "A Participant Observation Study of a Brain Injured Person Unable to Move or Speak." She slowly and reluctantly practices moving and speaking. Procrastination, artist's block or sloth and torpor? Whatever, she's younger now.

Devreaux Baker is the author of a book of poetry *Light At the Edge*. Her individual poems have been widely published in such places as *High Plains Literary Review*, *The American Voice*, *The Bloomsbury Review*, *Borderlands*, and *The Pacific Review*. In 1994 she received a Macdowell Fellowship and a Hawthornden Castle International Writers Award for poetry.

Johanna M. Bedford was born in 1949 and raised in Utrecht, Holland. She graduated from the University of Utrecht with a degree in history. At the age of twenty-three, she married and moved to the United States where she raised her two daughters. Her lifetime love affair with books began at sixteen when she got her first job selling books. Currently, she lives in Albion, California, where she gardens, paints and works in a local bookstore.

Zida Borcich, mother of two daughters, Zoé, 24, and Alicia, 18, has lived in Fort Bragg for over twenty-five years. She owns Zida Borcich Letterpress, a famous letterpress printshop and design studio, and *Studio Z Mendocino*, her line of fine letterpress correspondence papers that is sold nationally. She adores her children, words, typography, design, friends, her work, great food, dancing, travel, singing the blues, and free diving. In between, she writes the occasional poem.

Karin M. Bruhner was born in Colombia, South America on June 7, 1963. She was raised in the Bay Area, lived in Sweden, was married, moved to San Diego, had two children (now angels), was divorced and has moved most recently to Fort Bragg. Writing is the depth of her self-expression.

(handwritten in margin: Mendo Writers Conf.)

Suzanne Hartman Byerley's short stories and poems have appeared in commercial and literary magazines and she is winner of a Hopwood Award in fiction and a Fulbright in journalism. She teaches creative writing for College of the Redwoods in Mendocino and directs the Mendocino Coast Writers Conference. She lives in Fort Bragg with her husband and four cats and writes on Fridays.

Annie Correal spent part of her youth in Colombia, South America, before moving to the north coast, where she graduated in 1998 from Mendocino High School. She is now a freshman at Princeton University.

Maluma Crone has lived in Mendocino for more than ten years. Writing has been her creative outlet since second grade, but it was not until recently that she called herself a writer. She lives in the Willits hills with her partner of four and a half years and their dog and cat. She has recently taken up sculpting to reach those places that are beyond words.

Cecile Cutler is a yogini whose main concern is playing with the modality of yoga and yogic arts. What does this mean? Because she has found that the pursuit of yoga has opened the pathways of self inquiry/self awareness/self discovery, she has learned that she is not who she thought she is. There is NO fixed picture of who she is — because when she looks at who she is, sometimes there is nobody there. This frees her to continue to create herself.

In a practical sense, Cecile makes her living as a masseuse and teacher of yoga and qigong. Besides writing and designing, her favorite pursuit is digging holes for planting herbs and trees. Poetry comes in the night as dream and inspiration!

Janet DeBar was born in 1937 and raised in the northern panhandle of West Virginia. She attended the College of Wooster in Ohio, where she tried to resist the influence of Presbyterianism, and Stanford in California where she tried to resist the influence of Ivor Winters. She married in 1960 and supported her husband in the style of the '50s, living a rather goliardic existence: auditing classes in Latin at Berkeley and printing with William Everson at U.C. Santa Cruz. She was lucky enough to help with Everson's magnificent reliquary for Jeffers, *Granite and Cypress,* and she continued to work at the Lime Kiln Press until Everson's retirement. She and her husband have lived on the bluffs near Gualala for the past eleven years where she scubas under the opacity of their life-rich north coast water. Last year she began to backpack to give Earth her just due. Her current dream is to hike the whole of the Pacific Crest Trail.

Sharon Doubiago is the author of three book-length poems, *Hard Country, South America Mi Hija* (nominated twice for National Book Award), and *The Husband Arcane, The Arcane of O* (Gorda Plate Press, 1996). Her collection of poems *Psyche Drives the Coast* won the Oregon Book Award (1991), and her two collections of short stories, *The Book of Seeing With One's Own Eyes* and *El Niño,* are both in their second printings. The poems here are from her new manuscript *Body and Soul.* She considers the entire west coast her home, with Mendocino as base.

Kate Dougherty is a writer, mother, and in-home health care aid. She has published broadsides, cards and books with Dougherty Designs and is now co-editor of Front Porch Press. *The Elk*

Poems, a chapbook published by Pygmy Forest Press in 1989, now has a second printing with Front Porch Press. Kate teaches poetry to students in the county and co-hosts The Wild Sage Poetry Show on public radio station KZYX.

Julia Doughty is a poet, playwright, and editor of women's writing anthologies. She has taught writing courses in community colleges and schools throughout California, and leads workshops for women. As a Witter Bynner Foundation for Poetry grant recipient, she has taught writing classes for women survivors of violence.

Dana Ecelberger is a Virginia native transplanted to the northern coast of California where she is a gardener and single parent, part-time student and squeezing into the cracks of life writer. She has been published in *The Todd Point Review*, *The Hollins Critic*, *The Lucid Stone*, *The Mendonesian*, *The Memo*, *Sojourn Magazine*, and *Messages From the Heart*. A limited edition chapbook of her poetry and prose, *Beyond the Barricades*, was published by Rain Straight Down Press in 1996 and immediately sold out.

Liselotte Erlanger-Glozer has lived in Mendocino for thirty-four years. Her poems and stories have appeared in little magazines, locally as well as nationally. She won an Anna Davidson Rosenberg award for a poem on the Jewish experience. The poem "Ripening" has appeared in the *Connecticut Review*.

Karin Faulkner wrote her first book of poems at age four. It was about butterflies. After teaching with California Poets in the Schools for eighteen years in Mendocino county, this year she will finish her first novel, *Dog Song*, in Bali.

Sarah Flowers is a naturalist for coastal California State Parks. She instructs school programs in poetry and in natural history for the California Native Plant Society. Sarah's poems have appeared in many publications.

Cynthia Frank, president/publisher of QED Press, Cypress House and Lost Coast Press, and co-founder of Rain Straight Down Poetry and New Performance, has twenty years experience in writing, publishing, editing and teaching. She is the author of *A Sea-Lulled Rocky Mountain Isle* and co-author (with Hannes Krebs) of *A Mendocino Portfolio*. In her "spare" time she plays with her nine-year-old foster son, co-conducts the 50-voice Mendocino Women's Choir, and makes a darn good focaccia.

Susan Bowness Fraser was born and raised in southern California, the San Gabriel Valley to be specific, and is old enough to recall a small-town, fairly rural setting from her childhood. Condos have long since replaced the fields of wild mustard that were abundant in the area where she grew up and attended school. After attending college, marrying, and giving birth to a son in San Diego, she lived for a brief period in Mammoth Lakes, after which she ended up by chance as a single parent in the San Joaquin Valley, from which she escaped after teaching at a juvenile hall for thirteen years and at a community college (creative writing and psychology) for two years. She arrived on the Mendocino coast in 1985, and not even death itself will be able to budge her from this place. She is a school counselor and a therapist in private practice. Her poetry has always been her therapy. She lives in Mendocino with three slightly neurotic cats.

Jenny Gealey was killed in an accident June 3, 1995, at the end of her freshman year of high school just five days shy of her fifteenth birthday. Writing was Jenny's passion — and her dream. She filled journal after journal with poetry, prose, and daily musings. A selection of Jenny's earlier poetry appeared in *Purple Sky Flowers*, a collection she originally self-published with Karin Faulkner in the 7th grade through a California Poets in the Schools project. *Purple Sky Flowers* was reprinted by Faulkner's Rain Straight Down Press in 1996. Jenny's family has plans to one day compile another book which will include selections from journals, dream journals, short stories and poems written during the last three years of her life.

Liz Haapanen is a photographer, writer, potter and co-publisher of *Sojourn Magazine*. She has a degree in English literature from the University of California at Santa Barbara. She lives with her teenage son in Fort Bragg.

Julia Butterfly Hill has lived for nearly one year atop the ancient redwood tree, Luna, near the town of Stafford, California; the 1000 year-old tree, also known as the Stafford Giant, was marked for death by the Pacific Lumber Company. Julia's life with Luna began on December 10, 1997, when she ascended 180 feet to a makeshift platform high in Luna's branches in an effort to save Her and awaken the world to the destruction occuring to our old growth forests and hence, to the very quality of our lives. As this book goes to print, Luna and Julia still stand strong in defiance of destruction and oppression, and in defense of what is true, real and important. "This experience has opened me to the amazing power of unconditional love," says Julia, "with love all things are possible." Her poem, *Offerings to Luna*, was written as she witnessed the logging of the surrounding forest while living in her treetop home.

Nancy Horrocks grew up in a small town in upstate New York. She spent her 20s studying, working and wandering the world, eventually settling, in 1968, on Potrero Hill in San Francisco. On pure whim, she took part in a women's poetry writing seminar given by Kathleen Fraser in the early '80s and has never stopped writing. She and her son fell in love with Mendocino county and moved to Willits in 1988. Nancy sings with the Inland Valley Women's Chorus combining poetry with their music for concerts.

Diane Johnson has retired — again — and gone back to work writing and volunteering. She has lived among the Mendocino redwoods since 1984.

Patricia Olive Karch has lived in northern California all her life. She grew up, went to school and got married in the Bay Area. She and her family moved to Mendocino twenty-four years ago. She fell in love with small town life and the power of the forest and the ocean. She and her husband have a house in the pygmy forest which they designed and partially built themselves. They have raised their two daughters here. Patricia works at Comptche School and began writing poetry seven years ago at age 49 when a "poet in the schools" came to work with the kids. Poetry is her way of expressing what she could not otherwise express.

Lorel Kay wrote her first poetry while growing up in southern California. She has lived in northern California ever since she studied chemistry at U.C. Berkeley. One husband, three children, five grandchildren, and four technical professions (including teaching math and science) later, she now has prose pieces appearing in local Mendocino papers, but still puts the truly emotional experiences into poems.

Eleanor Kellner is a retired first-grade teacher, a perennial student, and a member of the National Association for Poetry Therapy. As an active volunteer she has brought the healing power of poetry to senior citizens through her leadership of groups in nursing homes, hospitals and day care centers. A lifelong lover of poetry, nurtured from infancy by her poetry-loving mother, she continues to write. Her poems have appeared in *Todd Point Review, Common Thread, Coast Magazine, Eve's Legacy* and *Lips Magazine.*

Carol Sanner Kohli is an honors graduate of the University of California at Berkeley, Columbia University School of Social Work, and a Phi Beta Kappa member. She is experienced in a variety of mind-body modalities and spiritual traditions. Her private practice in consciousness-oriented psychotherapy is located in Ukiah and Willits. She writes for *Sojourn* and *Confluence,* both Mendocino county publications. She is currently working on a book entitled *Body of Work: A Woman's Body Speaks its Truth.*

Mary Norbert Körte has in the course of the quarter-century lived in the redwood forest—a temperate rain forest—looked daily out the same kitchen window at the Noyo River carrying the silt of logged mountainsides to the Pacific Ocean at Fort Bragg, California. She has seen the woods around her decimated by the poisoning called chemical management; she has seen the salmon and steelhead struggle to reach spawning grounds blocked by culverts, slides, and other detritus of a technological society; she has seen exotic species of flora and fauna invade and destroy the native species. She has struggled constantly to find her place in these woods, and has tried to make her human marks lightly, lightly.

Ever since the early 1970s when she (along with a large audience) was warned by Gary Snyder not to be complacent ("The bulldozers are coming down your road, too," he said), she has felt that the woods must be protected most passionately by those who live in and with them. In Mendocino county, this is common practice: to defend the woods where your place is, and to live harmoniously with all woods people—those who make their living harvesting natural resources, as well as those to whom such extraction is anathema.

Many of us have worked hard to achieve this goal: understand the positions of the workers and their need to feed their families, yet never accede to the wholesale extraction of that home that is our heritage. She hopes that society at large will adopt this same goal before it is too late for the earth, the sky, the creatures—persons all—who dwell together.

Leah Leopold had written and published poetry as a young woman and then, due to illness, did not write for many years. While living in Elk in 1975, she began healing and again writing. After receiving a grant from the National Endowment for the Arts, she had a chapbook, *Echoes and Dreams,* published. A disabled veteran, she has also written some stories relating to her experiences.

Kay Lieberknecht's favorite tool is a shovel, and horses maintain the meaning in her life. Mud, ticks and stickers are constant motivators. Out a dirt road, up many hills, with six or eight horses, a couple of dogs, five cats, Chevy the goat, and Chicken Livered, she ekes out a frugal living with her partner and her teenage daughter. Kay and her partner are building their house and writing books. They share healing and joy via their business Hoofin' It: Custom Horse Adventures. Kay works as a nurse/massage therapist and she facilitates support groups for grieving and healing people. Poetry writes itself while she works, rides or drives, and she just has to record it.

M.L. Harrison Mackie is passionate about fly fishing and poetry. Comptche's redwoods are sanctuary for publishing, partnering and pondering what's next. Her mother, children and grandchildren are important parts of the puzzle constantly being taken apart and reassembled to shape life at sixty.

Susan Maeder's fiction has been widely published, and her one-woman show *Black Tulips* was produced in 1996. She lives in Mendocino. Pot Shard Press recently published *White Song*, her first collection of poems. She is co-editor of this anthology.

Stephanie MacLean lives on the north coast, has been writing since childhood, and had her first poem published at age seven. Stephanie has a master's in writing from the University of San Francisco and is currently at work on a collection of short stories and a novel about a north coast man.

Bobby Markels is a mother of two, a writer/performer and a thirty-year resident of Mendocino. She has taught creative writing and performance art and published many stories, poems and articles. She is the author of five books: *The Mendocino Malady* series, *Popper*, and *How To Be a Human Bean*. She has written and performed in two solo shows: *How I Got To Be World Famous Between Fort Bragg and Albion* and *This Is Not a Rehearsal*.

Anna Tui McCarthy was born in 1949 and raised in Nicaro, Oriente, Cuba. She attended Vassar, Laney and Mendocino Colleges and studied mushrooms at the College of the Redwoods. She arrived in Comptche in 1970 by way of Maine, New York State, England, Turkey, and Chicago. She currently practices herbalism, hypnotherapy and homeopathy in Willits and Garberville where she hopes to finish her northern California herbal novel soon.

Patricia Moore is a native Californian, born in the San Francisco Bay Area. She taught high school French for thirty-three years before retiring to the Mendocino coast in 1993. She loves opera, the San Francisco Giants and is an ardent francophile. Her favorite activity since retiring is being a classical music DJ for KZYX–Z, Mendocino county's public radio station.

Blake More is a performance poet and yogic dancer. She has put together numerous one-woman shows and performed in clubs and theaters in Tokyo, Los Angeles, New York City, San Francisco, and in Marin, Sonoma, and Mendocino counties. However since she has yet to find a way for such escapades to pay her bills, she currently earns a living as a freelance writer. She contributes monthly to *Yoga Journal* and writes a weekly yoga column on the Internet. To date, she has written two books. The non-fiction *The Definitive Guide To Headaches* is widely available at bookstores and health food stores, and *New Age Anonymous: Twelve Steps For Recovering New Agers* is her humorous look at new agers. She has nearly finished with her third and fourth books. *Bare Union*, poetry and yoga images, will be published by an independent press in Sausalito in the spring of 1999. *The Photon Connection: The Final Frontier of Nutrition*, will also be available in 1999.

Linda Noel is a California Native of the Koyungkowi Maidu tribe. She resides in Mendocino county.

Wendy Norris has been a resident of Mendocino county since 1980, except for five years at Mills College in Oakland where she earned a degree in art and anthropology. She is a California Poet in the Schools and is active in the Willits Community Theater. Her poetry has been published in anthologies and heard on KZYX public radio. She will celebrate her 30th birthday in June of 2000.

Mary Bradish O'Connor lives with her partner, two dogs, and two cats in a small house near the ocean. Every day, rain or shine, she is grateful for the grove of redwood trees in her back yard. Like a whale accumulates barnacles, she has accumulated life experiences as a psycho-therapist, editor, Latin teacher, professional grooming instructor, dean of students, wife, person with cancer, lesbian, book critic and country woman. She has two books of poems, *Calabash*, a collaboration, and *Say Yes Quickly*.

Patricia O'Donnell is the mother of three grown children, was married for twenty-four years, then not. She is an artist by profession but turned to writing in 1986 when she needed to convert her studio into a bedroom for her elderly dad. Dad's gone now and she has her studio back but she is still writing.

Rene W. Oschin, has sought peace of mind ever since she can remember. Fortunately she finds it often now. Her writings revolve around her relationship with nature and the nature of people. When she writes, she is exploring her heart.

Fionna Perkins is a poet, writer, and thirty-five year resident of the south Mendocino coast. She started the first bookstore in the village of Mendocino in 1960 and was one of the founders of the Coast Community Library in Point Arena in 1989. Her poem, "Hard Times for Women," written and read for the 75th Anniversary of Women's Right-to-Vote Day, August 26, 1995 in Mendocino, is now in a new anthology, *At Our Core: Women Writing About Power*. Her work is also in *Saltwater, Sweetwater*, a new collection of poems, stories, essays and memoirs by north coast women poets and writers.

Tracy Porterfield was born in northern California. She moved to Mendocino in September of '97 for clean air and open spaces. Her poetry and prose have been published locally. She is a contributing editor of *MendoScene* in which her work is regularly published. She recently earned her BA in English Literature, which began at the College of Marin and finished at UCLA.

Catherine Potenza was born in Oakland, California/ where sunsets on the Golden Gate/ cast purple rainbows into grey/ Life has been a poem ever since/ Now she is a noble grandmother/ She lives in Mendocino

Lydia Rand was born in Paris, France. Her first book of poetry was published by the St-Germain-des-Pré Press in that city. After traveling around the world she settled in the U. S. in the '60s and began writing in English. She came to the Mendocino area in 1970. A poetic memoir of childhood in occupied France was published by the Ten Mile River Press and a collection of poems by Pygmy Forest Press. She has contributed articles, poems and stories to numerous local and national literary journals, magazines and anthologies. She has also written collaboratively with other women writers, both fiction and non-fiction pieces. She is currently finishing a novel titled *Entre Nous.*

Jane Reichhold has been writing and publishing articles as a free-lancer in America and Europe since 1966. The range has been from Mennonite Church literature to homosexual magazines with art zines in the middle. All was done to feed the poetry habit. She is probably best known for the haiku, tanka and renga in her seventeen books, but still she writes and publishes other genres. As founder of AHA Books, co-editor of *Lynx*, and sponsor of the Tanka Splendor Awards, Jane has been instrumental in the introduction of tanka to English writers. This wide range of abilities and attitudes comes to fruition on her classic retro web page at: http://www.faximum.com/AHA!POETRY. She has lived in Mendocino county since 1981.

Helen Reynolds was born in Fergus Falls, Minnesota in 1910. From age eight through high school, she lived in Lodi, California. She graduated from U.C. Berkeley with a major in art and continued in graduate school for teachers' credentials and a Masters Degree in Art. She married Embree Reynolds in 1934, and spent post-WW II years with him in Vienna, Austria and Sendai, Japan. Since moving to Mendocino in 1969, she has been a print-maker and painter — and a "thinker in haiku."

Jess River came to Mendocino county thirty years ago and has written her way through the usual and unusual coastal casualties and celebrations. She is author of *Dwelling, On Making Your Own*, and was a founding member of the "Country Women" magazine editorial collective. Periodically, she teaches through the California Poets in the Schools program, and is currently at work on a collection of poems and a mountainous memoir.

Joan Meyersieck Rosen is both an artist and a poet. An environmental photographer with *Farming on the Edge* to her credit (U.C. Press), she has exhibited her work both in the United States and in France. She loves to travel the world, but has had roots in Comptche since 1965— where she does most of her writing, some of which was published locally in *Ridge Review* and *The Mendonesian.*

Robin Rule, 1989–90 recipient of a California Arts Council Fellowship in Literature, is the author of *Porch Language; The Drowning and Other Stories; Baseball Prayers; These Tattoos; Dogs of Pompei; The String Creek Saga; Crazy Sugar and Other Stories* and is currently working on *The Red*

Hill Poems.

Virginia Sharkey is a painter. She was born and raised in the midwest, graduated from Vassar College and had a studio in New York City for eleven years and in the Italian Alps before romance led her to McNab Ranch in the hills south of Hopland in 1981. She has lived on the coast since 1988. Her work has been exhibited in galleries and museums in New York, St. Louis, San Francisco and Germany. She teaches violin and performs regularly in local symphony and chamber music groups. She plans for her first book, a satire entitled *I'm Not Skitty-Cat!, The Unauthorized Autobiography,* to be published soon.

Shauna L. Smith is a licensed marriage and family therapist and author of *Making Peace With Your Adult Children: A Guide to Family Healing* (HarperCollins). She was a resident at the Mendocino Art Center for part of 1998 where she focused on writing short stories and poetry and worked in clay and watercolor. Shauna has two daughters and she and her husband maintain a private practice in Sacramento.

Joan Stanford has lived and worked on the north coast since 1980. Having grown up in Winnipeg, Canada where winters are long and harsh with plenty of snow, she has never taken this beautiful place for granted. To work and walk amidst such beauty is humbling and inspiring. She is an innkeeper, mother, wife, student, art therapist (almost), and committed to the creative process as a healing and spiritual path.

Judy Summers was born in Corpus Christi, Texas 11-14-39. She adored the spoken word, feared the spoken word, and came to poetry late in her teens, not counting nursery rhymes and song. She longs for the inspiration and time to write and holds her hand out for the gift.

Lourdes (Mary) Thuesen, poet, photographer and teacher, is a fourth generation San Franciscan. For many years she taught English literature in high schools in California. In 1979 she went to Altiplano of Peru where she lived and worked with the Aymara Indian people on the shores of Lake Titicaca. After eleven years, she returned to Mendocino county where she taught language arts and social studies in the middle school in Point Arena. Her work is regularly published by Luna Press.

Kathy Watson has always lived on the Mendocino coast. Her ancestors settled here before the turn of the century. She and her husband have two daughters who come and go on their various adventures, always returning to fill their home with joy. Her family is her inspiration.

ruth weiss lives in Albion on the north coast of California with her lover, artist Paul Blake. For more information check out the 1996 Contemporary Authors Autobiography Series, volume 24 (available only in libraries) and online Left Coast Art Magazine: www.leftcostart.com. Her most recent book, *For These Women of the Beat,* was published by 3300 Press in 1977.

Kate White spent her first eighteen years above the fog on Greenwood Ridge and has since been in and out of it. Albion is her home for the moment. She is a California Poets in the

Schools poet/teacher who loves to work with at-risk teenagers. In the summer months she is a gardener.

Theresa Whitehill, poet and graphic designer, trained as a letterpress printer and book designer at Mills College in the early 1980s, lives in Elk on the Mendocino coast, where she is editing a collaborative novel, *Metamorphio's Café*, which she wrote with three other Mendocino coast women. Recent published work includes articles on Portugal and California for *Appellation Magazine*, a poetry chapbook, *A Natural History of Mill Towns*, published by Pygmy Press, and *Diosas*, a suite of broadsides in collaboration with Sophia Sutherland. In the spring of 1998, she lived as Poet-in-Residence at Stag's Leap Winery in the Napa Valley, a project which will be on display at the Napa Valley Museum in Yountville in January of 1999. The literary broadsides of Colored Horse Studios can be found in collections of Brown University, the New York Public Library, the San Francisco Library, UCLA Special Collections, and the Los Angeles Public Library. http://www.coloredhorse.com

PERMISSIONS

SHARON DOUBIAGO: "Deer," *Rain City Review* (1997); "Ladene," *The Mendonesian* (1997); "The Unspeakable Commune of Our Soul" and "My Brother's Keeper," *Temple* (1997). Reprinted by permission of the author.

KATE DOUGHERTY: "Lazarus Moon," CNS NEWS & FEATURES, http://www.coastnews.com

DANA ECELBERGER: "Feral Cat," "After the Fact" and "A Mouth Full," *Beyond the Barricades* (Rain Straight Down, 1996). Reprinted by permission of the author.

LISELOTTE ERLANGER-GLOZER: "Ripening," *The Connecticut Review*. Reprinted by permission of the author.

JENNY GEALEY: "Child's Wheel," *Purple Sky Flowers.* (Rain Straight Down, 1996)

DIANE JOHNSON: "Stuff" (Third Thursday Poets). Reprinted by permission of the author.

M. L. HARRISON MACKIE: "What Else Can a Mother Tell Her Son?," *Lynx*. Reprinted by permission of the author.

SUSAN MAEDER: "Love Demands," "What We Need," "jasmine," "If the Trees Say Yes," "White Song II," "Why Now the River?" and "Danger," *White Song* (Pot Shard Press, 1998) Reprinted by permission of the author.

BOBBY MARKELS: "Mendocino Malady," *Mendocino Malady 4*. Reprinted by permission of the author.

LINDA NOEL: "Maybe They Couldn't Make the Shoe Fit" and "Independence Day," *The Newsletter Interview;* "Untitled," *Sojourn Magazine*. Reprinted by permission of the author.

WENDY NORRIS: "Water," *Something Like Homesickness* (Zapizdat Publications, 1997). Reprinted by permission of the author.

MARY BRADISH O'CONNOR: "Pah Tempe," and "Say Yes Quickly," *Say Yes Quickly* (Pot Shard Press, 1997); "Present Moment, Only Moment," *Calabash* (Pot Shard Press, 1997). Reprinted by permission of the author.

FIONNA PERKINS: "Choice," *The GAB*, June 1993. Reprinted by permission of the author.

TRACY PORTERFIELD: "Blue Room," *Todd Point Review*. Reprinted by permission of the author.

JANE REICHHOLD: "Live Dancing," *Raw Nervz*, Canada, "Original Colors," *Lynx*, "Dressed To Kill," and "Light Moon," *Mendocino Commentary;* "Passover," *SIJO West*. Reprinted by permission of the author.

HELEN REYNOLDS: "Untitled," *Modern Haiku*. Reprinted by permission of the author.

ROBIN RULE: "II," "III," "IV," "VII," and "VIII," *Dogs of Pompei*. Reprinted by permission of the author.

RUTH WEISS: "June 23rd, 1988/Anna Akhmatova," *Single Out* (D'Aurora Press, 1978); "Listen Papa" and "Mother's Day," *The Kerouac Connection* (September 1998); "Flame," *Womb Magazine*; "Carol," *Sojourn Magazine* (Issue #2, 1997); "Bonnie" *The Mendonesian*. Reprinted by permission of the author.

THERESA WHITEHILL: "Thirst," *The Mendonesian*; "O," *Upriver Downriver* (Petrolia, CA: Planet Drum Foundation, #17, '95) page 24; "Stealing Firewood," *Mendocino Review*, "Eucharist," *Semi-dwarf Quarterly* (Eureka, CA: Leonard J. Cirino, Volume 3, No. 2, Summer '98) page 46; "Hawai'ian Cement," *Oxygen No. 17* (San Francisco, CA: Richard Hack, March '97) pages 27–29; "Blurring," *The Mendonesian* (Mendocino, CA: Mike L. Evans, April '97) page 18; "Cinderella II (for Garlon)," *Semi-dwarf Quarterly* (Eureka, CA: Leonard J. Cirino, Winter '98) forthcoming. Reprinted by permission of the author.

INDEX
Authors *Titles* First lines

COLOPHON

The types used in this book are Monotype's Centaur family, including the Expert set, Centaur Festive Italic and Sorts.

The book is printed on Author's Natural Recycled stock (85% recycled, 10% post-consumer) and was printed and bound by Data Reproductions Corporation in Auburn Hills, Michigan.